ished in
ciation with
National
rait Gallery
Smithsonian Books
Washington, DC

PORTRAIT

Men and Women Who Have Shaped America Highlights from the Smithsonian's National Portrait Gallery

OF A NATION

Contents

The National Portrait Gallery:
The Place to Explore American Identity

Now more than ever, the National Portrait Gallery is a place to expect the unexpected. Of course, the museum includes some of the people, artworks, and themes that you would anticipate, such as "America's Presidents"; "American Origins"; "Twentieth-Century Americans"; "The Struggle for Justice"; a room titled "One Life," dedicated to the biography of one person; and "Champions" and "BRAVO!," focused on sports and the performing arts. But we also have a strong program of new art that aims to both reinforce our love of American traditions and challenge our assumptions of the past.

We're constantly updating the Portrait Gallery's offerings to reflect America—*all of America*—through the intersection between history, biography, and artistic expression. We put a human face on knowledge, culture, and identity by using portraiture to connect people across time, and to one another.

Congress established the Portrait Gallery in 1962, and the museum opened to the public in 1968. Its charter was to collect and display images of "men and women who have made significant contributions to the history, development and culture of the people of the United States." Think of the National Portrait Gallery as the ultimate meeting place where poets and presidents, visionaries and villains, actors and activists from our collective history come together to help explain the past and hint at the future. In *Portrait of a Nation*, you'll not only meet George Washington and George Washington Carver but also Pocahontas, Lucretia Mott, Annie Oakley, Michael Jordan, Spike Lee, Pedro Martinez, Colin Powell, Brad Pitt, and Maya Lin. With these glimpses into their lives and those who portrayed them, you'll get a perspective on how America has been shaped by its people—and hopefully become inspired to make your own mark.

Our collecting range encompasses a wide variety of media. We have not only paintings, sculpture, photographs, drawings, and

prints but also, increasingly, new media. You'll see a video still of George Clooney (see p. 296) from Lincoln Schatz's *Portrait of the Twenty-First Century* (which Schatz made for *Esquire* magazine in 2008), as well as Karen Sander's three-dimensional body scan of architect Maya Lin (see p. 308), done in 2014. On the other extreme, we have the historically significant *"Lansdowne"* painting of George Washington (see p. 30)—the most iconic portrait of America's first president. Our Frederick Hill Meserve collection of historical glass-plate negatives (some 5,400 objects) is represented by another icon—our "cracked-plate" image of Abraham Lincoln from February 1865 (see p. 88), one of the last photographs taken of him.

Adding to the breadth and depth of the collection are more than two thousand works of *Time* magazine original cover art, much of which was a gift of the original American weekly news magazine founded in 1923. This collection has enabled us to include people in the collection regardless of their nationality—hence Gerald Scarfe's wonderful mixed-media sculptures of the Beatles (see p. 218) from 1967.

The National Portrait Gallery is not just about fame and achievement. It is also about notoriety and disappointment; people who have made "significant contributions" can have a positive or negative impact. Whilst *Men of Progress* (see p. 80)—an 1862 representation of nineteen American scientists and inventors who "had altered the course of contemporary civilization" is pictured here, so is Abraham Lincoln's assassin, John Wilkes Booth (see p. 76).

These images in *Portrait of a Nation* are but a fraction of the works on view at the Portrait Gallery and in its collection. Come visit through this book, then in person or online. See who speaks to you, and see our world through a fresh set of eyes.

Kim Sajet
Director, National Portrait Gallery

Pocahontas, the Indian princess who allegedly saved the life of English colonist John Smith, survives and flourishes as an example of an early American heroine. Although Smith may have embellished the story of his rescue, the importance of Pocahontas to relations between colonists and Native Americans is undisputed. Following her conversion to Christianity and marriage to Englishman John Rolfe, Pocahontas journeyed to England with her family to demonstrate the ability of new settlers and Native tribes to coexist in the Virginia colony. She died at Gravesend, England, on her way back to Virginia.

While in England, she sat for her portrait, which was later engraved. That print served as the basis for this later portrait. The painter included an inscription beneath this likeness, copied from the engraving, but through an error in transcription misidentified her husband as Thomas, the name given to their son. ACG

Pocahontas (c. 1595–1617)

———

Unidentified artist, after Simon van de Passe
Oil on canvas, 77.5 × 64.8 cm (30½ × 25½ in.), after 1616
Gift of the A. W. Mellon Educational and Charitable Trust
NPG.65.61

Ætatis suæ 21. Aº. 1616.

Matoaks als Rebecka daughter to the mighty Prince
Powhatan Emperour of Attanoughkomouck als Virginia
converted and baptized in the Chriſtian faith, and
Wife to the worʳˡ Mʳ Tho: Rolff.

The Mohawk chief Etow Oh Koam was one of five Iroquois leaders to meet with Queen Anne and her court in April 1710. Accompanied by Colonel Pieter Schuyler, the mayor of Albany, this delegation traveled to London hoping to strengthen the tribe's political and trading alliance with England. Since the outbreak of Queen Anne's War in 1701, the French had been regularly raiding poorly protected English settlements in upstate New York. Although the Iroquois tribes had provided the English with some military assistance, the pleas of English colonists for help in this struggle had fallen largely on deaf ears back in England. Etow Oh Koam and his fellow delegates convinced Queen Anne to commit the resources to help defend the contested border, thereby hastening the war's end and formalizing an alliance that endured throughout much of the eighteenth century. FHG

Etow Oh Koam (life dates unknown)

————

John Simon (1675–c. 1755), after John Verelst
Mezzotint, 34.3 × 25.5 cm (13½ × 10⅟₁₆ in.), 1710
NPG.74.23

L. Verelst Pinx.ᵗ ETOW OH KOAM, King of the River Nation. I.Simon fecit.
Printed for Jnᵒ. Bowles & Son, at the Black Horse in Cornhill London.

2

In addition to bearing fourteen children, Anne Green helped her husband, Jonas, run the *Maryland Gazette*. When he died in 1767, she took over as manager of his printing shop and as the newspaper's editor. Under her supervision the enterprise thrived, and she gained a favorable reputation for recording opinions and events leading up to the American Revolution. During this period, she was also appointed the official printer of documents for the colony of Maryland. One of a small number of women printers during the colonial period, Green ran the newspaper for eight years.

In this portrait, among the first that Charles Willson Peale painted after returning from London in 1769, Peale represents Green not as her obituary recorded—a mother and wife of "a mild and benevolent Disposition…an Example of her Sex." Instead, he portrayed her as a professional printer with a copy of the *Maryland Gazette*, which announced Peale's return and included a notice about his portrait of William Pitt. SH

Anne Catharine Hoof Green (c. 1720–1775)

———————

Charles Willson Peale (1741–1827)
Oil on canvas, 91.4 × 71.1 cm (36 × 28 in.), 1769
Partial gift with funding from the Smithsonian Collections
Acquisitions Program and gift from the Governor's Mansion
Foundation of Maryland
NPG.91.152

Charles Cotesworth Pinckney posed for his portrait around 1773 in the red coat (traces of which remain) of the Charles Town (now Charleston, South Carolina) colonial militia. By 1775, despite formative years spent in England, Pinckney was an enthusiastic rebel. He asked artist Henry Benbridge to repaint the uniform, showing him as a captain in the Second South Carolina Regiment raised to fight the British. Pinckney, a friend remarked, had "a passion for glory and Zeal for the cause of his country."

Military glory eluded Pinckney—he was fated to participate in a string of defeats, never in victory—but seven years of faithful service won him the rank of brigadier general at the close of the war. Pinckney made his mark not as a soldier, but as a framer of the Constitution, an envoy to revolutionary France, and a Federalist presidential candidate. MCC

Charles Cotesworth Pinckney (1746–1825)

———

Henry Benbridge (1743–1812)
Oil on canvas, 76.7 × 64 cm (30³⁄₁₆ × 25³⁄₁₆ in.), c. 1773
NPG.67.1

Phillis Wheatley was the first African American to publish a book and the first American woman to earn a living from her writing, no small feat considering that she came to the colonies as a slave. Although most slaves had no opportunity for an education, within two years of Wheatley's purchase in 1761 she had learned to read and begun to write poetry. Her book, *Poems on Various Subjects, Religious and Moral* (1773), published in London, drew the praise of George Washington (see pp. 26 and 30), Benjamin Franklin (see p. 22), and Voltaire, and helped Wheatley gain her freedom. The frontispiece engraving emphasized Wheatley's demure appearance and creative intelligence. WWR

Phillis Wheatley (c. 1753–1784)

————

Unidentified artist
Engraving, 17.6 × 12.8 cm (6¹⁵⁄₁₆ × 5¹⁄₁₆ in.), 1773
NPG.77.2

PHILLIS WHEATLEY, NEGRO SERVANT to Mr. JOHN WHEATLEY, of BOSTON.

Published according to Act of Parliament, Sept.ʳ 1, 1773 by Arch.ᵈ Bell, Bookſeller Nᵒ. 8 near the Saracens Head Aldgate.

John Singleton Copley, proclaimed John Adams, was "the greatest Master, that ever was in America." Even as a teenager, Copley had the artistic ability to fulfill Bostonians' requests for realistic portraits; by the time he was twenty, the essentially self-taught artist was painting better pictures than he had ever seen. Frustrated by the limitations of his provincial environment, where people, he complained, generally regarded art as "no more than any other useful trade," Copley longed to go to Europe to study. Increased political turmoil in the wake of the Boston Tea Party of December 1773—his father-in-law was one of the merchants who were supposed to receive the tea dumped in the harbor—spurred his departure for England in June 1774. There, in the flush of new success, he painted his own likeness. He never returned to America. MCC

John Singleton Copley (1738–1815)

———————

Self-portrait
Oil on canvas, 56.5 cm (22¼ in.) diameter, 1780–84
Gift of The Morris and Gwendolyn Cafritz Foundation, with matching funds from the Smithsonian Institution
NPG.77.22

Benjamin Franklin, in his day the most famous American in the world, returned from his years representing colonial interests in England just in time to be unanimously elected to represent Pennsylvania at the Second Continental Congress. Behind him was a lifetime of achievement as a printer, an unsurpassed author of wit and wisdom, an inventor, and a scientist. Ahead were his roles as a signer of the Declaration of Independence and as a member of the Constitutional Convention of 1787. In between was his triumph as a diplomat in France, where this portrait was ordered by Madame Brillon de Jouy, who loved Franklin's "droll roguishness which shows that the wisest of men allows his wisdom to be perpetually broken against the rocks of femininity."

In 2013 this portrait was selected as the basis for Franklin's engraved image on the redesigned hundred-dollar bill. MCC

Benjamin Franklin (1706–1790)

———

Joseph Siffred Duplessis (1725–1802)
Oil on canvas, 72.4 × 59.7 cm (28½ × 23½ in.), c. 1785
Gift of The Morris and Gwendolyn Cafritz Foundation
NPG.87.43

Daniel Shays (left), a Revolutionary War captain, gave his name to the 1786–87 tax rebellion in western and central Massachusetts. Armed farmers, threatened with the loss of their farms and imprisonment for debt, forced the closing of the courts and marched upon the arsenal at Springfield. The militia was called out, the insurrection at length put down, most of the rebels pardoned (Shays fled to Vermont), and their grievances addressed by the state legislature. Most significantly, Shays' Rebellion frightened conservatives throughout the country and gave an urgency to the need for a stronger central government. Job Shattuck joined Shays as a leading figure in the rebellion. MCC

Daniel Shays (1747–1825)
Job Shattuck (1736–1819)

———

Unidentified artist
Relief cut, 9 × 12.9 cm (3⁹⁄₁₆ × 5¹⁄₁₆ in.), 1787
Published in *Bickerstaff's Boston Almanack for 1787*
(3rd edition, Boston)
NPG.75.25

Gen. DANIEL SHAYS. *Col.* JOB SHATTUCK.

Thro' dusted Storms let SHAYS the Court affail,
And SHATTUCK rife, illustrious from the Jail.
In coward Hands let legal Powers expire,
And give new Subjects to my founding Lyre.

American artist Gilbert Stuart was commissioned to paint this portrait after the success of his first portrait of George Washington in 1795. Martha Washington (see p. 28) convinced the president to sit again because, according to artist Rembrandt Peale, she "wished a Portrait for herself; he therefore consented on the express condition that *when finished* it should be hers." Stuart, however, preferred this portrait to his earlier *Washington*; he purposely left it, and that of the first lady, unfinished so that he could use this as a model for the numerous copies that the president's admirers commissioned. After Stuart's death, the two paintings were purchased for the Boston Athenaeum, which owned them for more than 150 years.

This image served as the basis for the engraving of Washington on the one-dollar bill. John Neal, an early-nineteenth-century writer and art critic, wrote, "Though a better likeness of him were shown to us, we should reject it; for, the only idea that we now have of George Washington, is associated with Stuart's Washington." FSV

"Athenaeum" portrait
George Washington (1732–1799)

————

Gilbert Stuart (1755–1828)
Oil on canvas, 121.9 × 94 cm (48 × 37 in.), 1796
Owned jointly with the Museum of Fine Arts, Boston
NPG.80.115

In 1749, Martha Dandridge married Daniel Parke Custis, the wealthiest planter in the Virginia colony. Seven years and four children later, she was a very wealthy widow. She married George Washington (see pp. 26 and 30) in 1759, pulling him upward in Virginia's social and economic strata. Martha's contemporaries viewed her as a quiet, reserved woman capable of managing an estate—a good match for an ambitious planter. During the Revolutionary War, Martha stayed with her husband in the Continental army's winter encampment; she was a great comfort to George and a major factor in his being able to keep the army intact. She was also, along with her husband, influential in setting the atmosphere and tone of the American presidency, which was so important to the new republic.

Gilbert Stuart painted this portrait of Martha Washington at the same time he did that of the president. These paintings, commissioned by the Washingtons, were never completed, and the artist kept them in his possession until his death. Although Stuart made many copies of the president's portrait, no other likeness of Martha Washington by Stuart is known to exist. SH/FSV

Martha Washington (1731–1802)

———

Gilbert Stuart (1755–1828)
Oil on canvas, 121.9 × 94 cm (48 × 37 in.), 1796
Owned jointly with the Museum of Fine Arts, Boston
NPG.80.116

George Washington basically "invented" the American presidency. Washington's presence at the Constitutional Convention of 1787 and the delegates' trust that he would not abuse power gave them the confidence to create a strong executive, notwithstanding their fear of kings. They all expected Washington to be the first president. In that office, Washington established many of the executive powers that presidents have today: executive privilege, authority to call out the National Guard in emergencies, establishing a cabinet. Washington even selected "Mr. President" as the title most suitable for the chief executive in a republic. He also established the unofficial two-term limit, which he considered an essential check on executive power; later, the Twenty-second Amendment (1951) made the two-term limit a part of the Constitution.

American-born Gilbert Stuart had spent eighteen years in Europe honing his artistry before he returned to the United States. He painted Washington several times in the mid-1790s (see p. 26). In 1796 Senator and Mrs. William Bingham of Pennsylvania commissioned Stuart to paint this portrait as a gift to the Marquis of Lansdowne, an English supporter of American independence. Stuart and others copied it as the definitive image of Washington. SH

"Lansdowne" portrait
George Washington (1732–1799)

————

Gilbert Stuart (1755–1828)
Oil on canvas, 247.6 × 158.7 cm (97 ½ × 62 ½ in.), 1796
Acquired as a gift to the nation through the generosity
of the Donald W. Reynolds Foundation
NPG.2001.13

Peace medals are an important part of the history of U.S. presidential portraiture and also an essential element in federal Indian policy. Presented to Native American chiefs on such important occasions as the signing of a treaty or a visit to the nation's capital, the medals gave rank and distinction, and many were passed down from generation to generation.

In the first half of the nineteenth century, the design of medals, such as this one of Thomas Jefferson, was determined by the need to win the allegiance of the Indians. Medals contained the likeness of the president on one side and symbols of peace and friend-ship on the other. Acceptance of a medal marked the Indians' friendship and loyalty to the United States. By midcentury, the peace medals encouraged assimilation of the Native Americans into American society. FSV

Peace medal
Thomas Jefferson (1743–1826)

————

Robert Scott (active 1781–1820)
Silver, 10.8 cm (4¼ in.) diameter, 1801
Gift of Betty A. and Lloyd G. Schermer
NPG.99.108

Thomas Jefferson's tombstone notes, by his own instruction, that he authored the Declaration of Independence, founded the University of Virginia, and was responsible for Virginia's Statute for Religious Freedom. But it fails to mention that this philosopher, inventor, and scientist was also president of the United States. This omission does not mean that his administration lacked significance. During Jefferson's presidency, the nation acquired from France the vast wilderness known as the Louisiana Purchase and successfully stood its ground against extortion attempts from Barbary Coast pirates in the Mediterranean. These early successes, however, paled in comparison to the wrath later heaped on Jefferson in the wake of the economically disastrous trade embargo he imposed in response to British and French interference with U.S. shipping. A much-beleaguered Jefferson ended his presidency by calling it a best-forgotten "splendid misery."

Gilbert Stuart was not only early America's most admired portraitist but also an eccentric known for procrastinating. After sitting for this portrait in 1805, Jefferson had to wait sixteen years before it was finally delivered. FSV

Thomas Jefferson (1743–1826)

———

Gilbert Stuart (1755–1828)
Oil on wood panel, 66.4 × 53.3 cm (26⅛ × 21 in.), 1805/1821
Owned jointly with Monticello, Thomas Jefferson Foundation, Inc., Charlottesville, Virginia; purchase funds provided by the Regents of the Smithsonian Institution, the Trustees of the Thomas Jefferson Foundation, Inc., and the Enid and Crosby Kemper Foundation
NPG.82.97

Although illegitimate and orphaned at an early age, Alexander Hamilton possessed the drive and intelligence that attracted wealthy patrons who sent him from his home in St. Croix to North America to study at King's College (now Columbia University). An early advocate for independence from Britain, he enlisted in the army and came to the attention of George Washington (see pp. 26 and 30), who made him a member of his military "family."

After independence, Hamilton supported a stronger national government, assisting in the ratification of the Constitution by authoring, with John Jay and James Madison, the most original contribution to American political thought, the *Federalist Papers*. Washington, impressed with Hamilton's mastery of economics, made him the first secretary of the treasury. Hamilton's policies— assumption of state debts, encouragement of commerce and manufacturing, and promotion of a national bank—are credited with laying the groundwork for a strong republic. He was killed in a duel with Thomas Jefferson's vice president, Aaron Burr. SH

Alexander Hamilton (1757–1804)

———

John Trumbull (1756–1843), after Giuseppe Ceracchi
Oil on canvas, 77.5 × 62.2 cm (30½ × 24½ in.), 1806
Gift of Henry Cabot Lodge
NPG.79.216

Thomas Paul

A pioneer in the establishment of independent black churches, Thomas Paul was educated at the Free Will Baptist Church in Hollis, New Hampshire, and came to Boston as an itinerant preacher. In August 1805 he led the effort to found the African Baptist Church, and by the end of the year a meetinghouse (which still stands as the oldest surviving black church building in America) was completed on Beacon Hill. During the next twenty-five years, Paul exerted strong leadership over a growing congregation and won fame as he expanded his missionary work. Famed diarist Rev. William Bentley of Salem went to hear Paul speak and recorded: "He impressed the audience with a regard to his sincerity & many with a sense of his talents. His person is good." MCC

Thomas Paul (1773–1831)

———

Thomas Badger (1792–1868)
Oil on wood panel, 20.3 × 16.5 cm (8 × 6½ in.), c. 1825
NPG.70.45

Seneca chief Sagoyewatha, a swift runner for the British during the American Revolution, was given the name "Red Jacket" for the scarlet coats he often wore. During the War of 1812, he cast his lot with the Americans, but after participating in several battles, including the Battle of Chippewa, he proposed that Indians fighting on both sides of the conflict withdraw from the war, and he went home.

Sagoyewatha's claim to celebrity was not as a warrior, but as an orator. An eloquent defender of Native American land claims and culture, he detested Christianity and white civilization. Nonetheless, in his many portraits he proudly wears the peace medal presented to him by President George Washington (see pp. 26 and 30) in 1792 when he went to Philadelphia to assert Seneca claims and grievances. MCC

Sagoyewatha (c. 1758–1830)

———

Thomas Hicks (1823–1890), after Robert W. Weir
Oil on canvas, 81.3 × 55.9 cm (32 × 22 in.), 1868 after 1828 original
NPG.2002.69

The career of Ira Aldridge illustrates the costs that racism inflicted on African Americans and on America itself. Aldridge was one of the great actors of his age—but he was black. Unable to work in America, he moved to England in the 1820s and lived abroad until his death. Aldridge's most famous role was Othello, in which he is shown here, a part that he invested with the poignancy of his own experience; a Russian critic wrote in 1858 that "he was Othello himself, as created by Shakespeare." Yet Aldridge was not bound by color in his acting. He played most of Shakespeare's main characters, especially the tragic heroes. Aldridge's career foreshadows the fate of many African American artists, such as dancer Josephine Baker or jazz musician Dexter Gordon, who had to go to Europe to find wide acclaim. DCW

Ira Aldridge (1805–1867)

————

Henry Perronet Briggs (c. 1791–1844)
Oil on canvas, 128.3 × 103.5 cm (50½ × 40¾ in.), c. 1830
NPG.72.73

Sequoyah, allegedly the son of a Cherokee chief's daughter and a fur trader from Virginia, was a warrior and hunter and, some say, a silversmith. For twelve years he worked to devise a method of writing the Cherokee language. His syllabary of eighty-six symbols, representing vowel and consonant sounds, was approved by the Cherokee chiefs in 1821, and the simple utilitarian system made possible a rapid spread of literacy throughout the Cherokee Nation. Traditional healers set down ceremonies for healing, divination, war, and traditional ball games; missionaries translated hymns and the New Testament into the Native language; and in 1828 the *Cherokee Phoenix,* a weekly bilingual newspaper, began publication at New Echota, Georgia.

The original portrait of Sequoyah, painted by Charles Bird King, was destroyed by the fire that swept through the Smithsonian Castle building in January 1865. MCC

Sequoyah (c. 1770–1843)

———

Henry Inman (1801–1846), after Charles Bird King
Oil on canvas, 76.8 × 64.1 cm (30 ¼ × 25 ¼ in.), c. 1830
NPG.79.174

Unlike Daniel Boone, his solitary predecessor in frontiersman lore, Davy Crockett created the image of a jocular, colorful "type" who loved tall tales, whiskey, and cutting a caper. Crockett was an inept farmer and kicked around the Southeast, serving in the military and minor governmental offices. On a whim he ran for Congress from Tennessee, serving two terms (1827–31 and 1833–35). To capitalize on his political fame, he penned an autobiography containing the motto "Be always sure you're right—then go ahead," which has been the credo of the frontiersman, in reality and myth, to the present day. After Congress, Crockett created a road show in which he presented himself to civilized eastern audiences as the wild and woolly backwoodsman, "half man, half alligator." Still restless, however, Crockett joined the fight for Texas independence and was killed at the Alamo. DCW

Davy Crockett (1786–1836)

———

Chester Harding (1792–1866)
Oil on canvas, 76.2 × 63.5 cm (30 × 25 in.), 1834
Future bequest of Ms. Katharine Bradford
L/NPG.1.88

If John C. Calhoun (see p. 56) was the South's leading advocate of states' rights, New England's Daniel Webster was easily its most celebrated opponent. Endowed with an imposingly broad brow that seemed to underscore his eloquence in the Senate and court-room, Webster was unmatched in his gift for speaking. In 1830 he held his audience enthralled as he turned an exchange with South Carolina senator Robert Hayne into a debate over states' rights. Ending his oration with "Liberty and Union, now and forever, one and inseparable," he left his listeners spellbound, and it was many minutes before any dared to speak. From that moment, Webster was for many a living emblem of national unity.

Francis Alexander painted this portrait in 1835 to commemorate Webster's role in an 1818 Supreme Court case that protected Dartmouth College's charter from being negated. JGB

Daniel Webster (1782–1852)

⸺

Francis Alexander (1800–1880)
Oil on canvas, 76.2 × 63.5 cm (30 × 25 in.), 1835
Bequest of Mrs. John Hay Whitney
NPG.98.71

Andrew Jackson of Tennessee, Indian fighter and hero of the Battle of New Orleans—the first president of truly humble background and the first from a western state (as Tennessee then was)—ushered in a new political era. His supporters hailed him as the "People's President"; conservatives saw his election as the ascent of "King Mob."

Before his two terms in office were out, Jackson had vetoed more legislation than the previous presidents combined. And unlike his predecessors, who invoked that power on strictly constitutional grounds, Jackson vetoed key congressional measures, not because he deemed them illegal, but simply because he did not like them. In doing so, he set a precedent that vastly enlarged the presidential role in congressional lawmaking.

Among Jackson's opponents, this executive activism drew charges of dictatorship. Those accusations, however, carried little weight among yeoman farmers and laborers, who affirmed Jackson's professed opposition to elitism. FSV

Andrew Jackson (1767–1845)

———

Ferdinand Pettrich (1798–1872)
Marble, 64.8 cm (25½ in.) height, replica of 1836 original
NPG.91.45

Cinqué was the slave name given to Singbe Pieh by the Spanish who illegally enslaved him and fifty-two others in 1839. While the slave ship *Amistad* sailed from one Cuban port to another, Cinqué led a successful mutiny aboard the ship. But the Africans then had to rely on a Spanish helmsman, who steered the ship to Long Island instead of back to Africa. U.S. authorities secured the *Amistad*, and the slaves were interned in New Haven, Connecticut. While the federal government, fearful of offending the South, wanted to recognize the law of property and return the slaves to their owners, the District Court in New Haven ordered them freed. When the government appealed, ex-president John Quincy Adams defended the *Amistad* prisoners before the U.S. Supreme Court, successfully arguing that the right of habeas corpus prohibited their illegal seizure. Cinqué and his fellow captives were returned to Africa. DCW

Cinqué (c. 1817–c. 1879)

———

John Sartain (1808–1897), after Nathaniel Jocelyn
Mezzotint, 23.2 × 19.1 cm (9⅛ × 7½ in.), c. 1840
NPG.69.66

Engraved by J. Sartain.

Cinque

His admirers called him "Gallant Harry," and his impetuous charm made him quite possibly the most beloved politician of his generation. But the real legacy of Kentucky's Henry Clay was his unstinting devotion, in the House of Representatives and later in the Senate, to maintaining a strong American union. In the early 1830s, as southern states threatened to nullify federal authority over a tariff bill that would have hurt plantation economies, Clay set aside his own preference for the new law to orchestrate a compromise. In 1850, with the North and South on the verge of armed conflict over the extension of slavery into the new western territories, Clay again stepped in with proposals that, temporarily at least, satisfied both sections. This last act of his career earned him the title of "Great Pacificator." JGB

Henry Clay (1777–1852)

———————

John Neagle (1796–1865)
Oil on canvas, 70.5 × 55.2 cm (27¾ × 21¾ in.), 1842
NPG.93.476

South Carolina's John C. Calhoun was a formidable presence in American politics for nearly four decades. During that time, he served twice as vice president and sat in two cabinets. It was during his later years in the Senate, however, that he had his greatest impact, as a champion of southern interests and formulator of a sectional doctrine of states' rights. But even as he defended the South against attempts to curb slavery and argued for the right of states to reject federal policies, he sensed that he was fighting a losing battle. His dying words in 1850 were "The South, the poor South."

One of five known versions of the likeness that artist G. P. A. Healy made from sittings with Calhoun in 1844, this portrait originally belonged to Calhoun himself. JGB

John C. Calhoun (1782–1850)

———

George Peter Alexander Healy (1813–1894)
Oil on canvas, 91.9 × 74.1 cm (36³⁄₁₆ × 29³⁄₁₆ in.), c. 1845
NPG.90.52

This earliest known portrait of radical abolitionist John Brown shows him standing with one hand raised, as if repeating his public pledge to dedicate his life to the destruction of slavery. With his other hand, he grasps what is believed to be the standard of his "Subterranean Pass Way"—the militant alternative to the Underground Railroad that Brown sought to establish in the Allegheny Mountains more than a decade before his ill-fated raid on the U.S. Army arsenal at Harpers Ferry in 1859.

Augustus Washington, the son of a former slave, first took up the camera to help fund his studies at Dartmouth College. In 1844 he accepted a teaching post in Hartford, Connecticut, where he established a daguerreotype studio and also wrote for antislavery journals. Washington and his family immigrated to the West African nation of Liberia in 1853, where he continued to make portraits. He also founded a newspaper, became a major sugarcane producer, and took an active role in Liberia's political affairs. AMS

John Brown (1800–1859)

———

Augustus Washington (1820/21–1875)
Quarter-plate daguerreotype, approx. 10 × 8.2 cm (4 × 3¼ in.), c. 1846–47
Purchased with major acquisitions funds and with funds donated
by Betty Adler Schermer in honor of her great-grandfather,
August M. Bondi
NPG.96.123

In the years following his escape from bondage in 1838, former slave Frederick Douglass emerged as a powerful and persuasive spokesman for the cause of abolition. Douglass's effectiveness as an antislavery advocate was due in large measure to his firsthand experience with the evils of slavery and his extraordinary skill as an orator. A correspondent from the *New Englander* noted that his "glowing logic, biting irony, melting appeals, and electrifying eloquence" astonished and enthralled his audiences. Convinced that a peaceful end to slavery was impossible, Douglass embraced the Civil War as a fight for emancipation and called upon President Abraham Lincoln (see p. 88) to enlist black troops in the cause.

As this daguerreotype suggests, Douglass's power was also rooted in the sheer impressiveness of his bearing, which abolitionist and activist Elizabeth Cady Stanton likened to that of "an African prince, majestic in his wrath." AMS

Frederick Douglass (1818–1895)

———

Unidentified photographer
Sixth-plate daguerreotype, approx. 8 × 6.9 cm (3⅛ × 2¹¹⁄₁₆ in.)
c. 1850 after c. 1847 original
NPG.80.21

Dolley Payne Todd Madison served as White House hostess during the administrations of the widowed Thomas Jefferson (see p. 34) and her own husband, James Madison. Her effervescence doubtless accounted, in part at least, for the popularity of Madison's presidency in its last several years. After the end of Madison's term in 1817, Dolley helped her husband put his papers in order, selling a portion of them to Congress after his death.

William Elwell painted Dolley Madison's portrait in February 1848 and later sold it to her longtime friend William Winston Seaton, editor and co-owner of the Washington, D.C., newspaper the *National Intelligencer*. The portrait offers a glimpse of the aging Mrs. Madison, described by the artist in his diary as "a very Estimable lady—kind & obliging—one of the Old School." FSV

Dolley Madison (1768–1849)

———

William S. Elwell (1810–1881)
Oil on canvas, 76.8 × 64.1 cm (30 ¼ × 25 ¼ in.), 1848
NPG.74.6

Showman Phineas Taylor Barnum was as skilled in promoting legitimate entertainment as he was in marketing outlandish frauds. In 1842, he scored one of his greatest triumphs when he discovered the diminutive Charles Stratton and introduced him to the public as "General Tom Thumb." The four-year-old Stratton, who was just twenty-five inches tall and weighed only fifteen pounds, was transformed under Barnum's tutelage into a phenomenally popular entertainer who sang, danced, and performed a variety of costumed roles. Memorialized in this double portrait, the long-lived and amiable partnership between General Tom Thumb and the "Prince of Humbug" generated substantial fortunes for both men. AMS

P. T. Barnum (1810–1891)
General Tom Thumb (1838–1883)

———

Attributed to Samuel Root (1819–1889) or Marcus Aurelius Root (1808–1888)
Half-plate daguerreotype, approx. 14 × 10.7 cm (5½ × 4³⁄₁₆ in.), c. 1850
NPG.93.154

Although scarcely more than twenty years old when he opened his first daguerrean gallery in New York City in 1844, Mathew Brady quickly earned accolades for his superior portraits. His clientele grew to include prominent men and women from every quarter, and his collection of images of the famous was soon unsurpassed. While daily studio operations remained the province of his camera operators and technicians, Brady provided the creative vision and marketing expertise that, by the time of the Civil War, made him the best-known photographer in America. This daguerreotype pictures Brady with his wife, Julia (left), and Mrs. Haggerty, Brady's sister. AMS

Mathew Brady (c. 1823–1896)
Juliet "Julia" Handy Brady (1822–1887)
Mrs. Haggerty (life dates unknown)

———

Unidentified photographer at the Mathew Brady Studio (active 1844–94)
Quarter-plate daguerreotype, 10.7 × 8.3 cm (4³⁄₁₆ × 3¼ in.), c. 1851
NPG.85.78

Lucretia Mott's commitment to ending slavery and securing rights for women became the defining features of her life. A devout Quaker whose activism proved unsettling to some members of her faith, Mott assumed a highly visible role in the abolitionist movement. After joining William Lloyd Garrison at the launch of the American Anti-Slavery Society in 1833, she helped to found Philadelphia's Female Anti-Slavery Society. Her concern for women's rights was a natural outgrowth of her abolitionist efforts, and in 1848 Mott and Elizabeth Cady Stanton organized the convention at Seneca Falls, New York, that gave birth to the women's suffrage movement. AMS

Lucretia Mott (1793–1880)

———

Marcus Aurelius Root (1808–1888)
Half-plate daguerreotype, 14 × 10.7 cm (5½ × 4³⁄₁₆ in.), 1851
NPG.2009.32

Lucretia Mott. Phila.   1851

Excluded from public professions, cultivated women sought other avenues for their talents. From discussing the issues of the day in informal salon gatherings, it was a short step for women to become writers, especially since the antebellum period saw a burgeoning number of magazines catering to women. So, Harriet Beecher Stowe started a career that made her one of the most popular novelists of the nineteenth century. Stowe's place in American history was sealed with her novel *Uncle Tom's Cabin* (1851–52), which sold three hundred thousand copies in its first year. *Uncle Tom's Cabin* was a reform novel; Stowe was motivated to write it by the Fugitive Slave Law and the effect that slavery had in destroying the African American family. No more effective charge could be made in a nation that, both North and South, revered the family as the foundation of society. **DCW**

Harriet Beecher Stowe (1811–1896)

————

Alanson Fisher (1807–1884)
Oil on canvas, 86.4 × 68.6 cm (34 × 27 in.), 1853
NPG.68.1

Described by a contemporary as "the apostle of individuality in an age of association and compromise," author Henry David Thoreau followed his own moral compass and lived a life largely unfettered by convention. In such works as *Walden* (1854) and "Civil Disobedience" (1849), Thoreau encouraged readers to question popular wisdom and to seek universal truths from simple facts. When an admirer wrote from Michigan in 1856 asking for Thoreau's daguerreotype and enclosing money to defray its cost, the author reluctantly obliged. A visit to Maxham's Daguerrean Palace yielded this 50-cent portrait, which Thoreau dutifully sent to the requestor along with $1.70 in change. AMS

Henry David Thoreau (1817–1862)

————

Benjamin D. Maxham (1821–1899)
Ninth-plate daguerreotype, approx. 6.3 × 4.7 cm (2½ × 1⅞ in.), 1856
Gift of an anonymous donor
NPG.72.119

In June 1861—just two months after the start of the Civil War—George Armstrong Custer graduated from the U.S. Military Academy at West Point and entered the Union army as a second lieutenant. One of the army's rising stars, Custer was only twenty-three when he became the youngest officer promoted to brigadier general, in 1863. By the war's end, his bravery and daring had earned him the rank of major general in Philip Sheridan's cavalry corps. After the war, he emerged as one of the most visible and controversial military leaders in the West. His victories in battles with the Cheyenne and Lakota tribes enhanced his reputation as an Indian fighter, even though accounts of the killing of Native women and children also led to accusations of misconduct. He met an early death at the Battle of the Little Bighorn in June 1876, when he and five companies under his command were wiped out by a force of two thousand Lakota warriors.

Custer was still a West Point cadet when he posed for this portrait holding his Colt pocket pistol. AMS / FHG

George A. Custer (1839–1876)

———

Unidentified photographer
Quarter-plate ambrotype, approx. 10.6 × 8.1 cm (4 3/16 × 3 3/16 in.), c. 1860
NPG.81.138

A member of one of America's most famous theatrical families, John Wilkes Booth was fiercely dedicated to the Confederate cause. By the final months of the Civil War, he had become obsessed with a deep hatred of President Abraham Lincoln (see p. 88). In late 1864, thinking that the southern cause could be salvaged with Lincoln out of the way, Booth conspired to kidnap the Union president and deliver him into Confederate hands in Richmond. After that scheme failed, he began plotting Lincoln's assassination. On the evening of April 14, 1865, his plan tragically unfolded when he fatally shot Lincoln as the president sat watching a play at Ford's Theatre in Washington, D.C. Despite breaking his leg as he escaped from the theater, Booth fled, first to Maryland, then across the Potomac River into Virginia. Union cavalrymen followed his trail to a barn near Port Royal, where he was shot and killed on April 26. JGB

John Wilkes Booth (1838–1865)

———

Charles DeForest Fredricks (1823–1894)
Coated salted-paper print, 22.5 × 17.5 cm (8 ⅞ × 6 ⅞ in.), c. 1862
NPG.2002.85

One of the enduring myths of America is that it has no history but exists in the liberating freedom of the present moment. Nathaniel Hawthorne's novels, fables, and "tales" were a cautionary lesson to Americans who ignored the past. (Hawthorne knew the more optimistic writers of the time but was friends with none of them.) His writings secularized the harsh Puritan worldview of his Salem birthplace to remind Americans that actions had consequences, both for individuals and communities. His novels turned on the clash of the individual will—from the lovers in *The Scarlet Letter* (1850) to the naive philanthropist of *The Blithedale Romance* (1852)—against the implacability of society and nature. Hawthorne's sympathies were often with his rebels, but his philosophy required their defeat. It was perhaps the irreconcilability of these viewpoints that led to his artistic decline in the 1850s. DCW

Nathaniel Hawthorne (1804–1864)

———

Emanuel Gottlieb Leutze (1816–1868)
Oil on canvas, 75.9 × 64.1 cm (29⅞ × 25¼ in.), 1862
Gift of the A. W. Mellon Educational and Charitable Trust
NPG.65.55

In 1857, the inventor of a coal-burning stove, Jordan Mott, commissioned Christian Schussele to paint a group portrait of eighteen other American scientists and inventors who "had altered the course of contemporary civilization." As with Schussele's celebration of American letters, *Washington Irving and His Literary Friends at Sunnyside*, the group portrait did not mark an actual occasion but was designed to honor the achievements of American industry. The artist sketched study portraits of each of his subjects before putting them all into his final, formal composition. *Men of Progress* is a remarkable document of the growth of the American economy by the 1850s, as it celebrates the inventions and processes of manufacturing pioneered by men such as Cyrus McCormick, Samuel Colt, and Elias Howe. DCW

Left to right: William T. G. Morton (1819–1868), James Bogardus (1800–1874), Samuel Colt (1814–1862), Cyrus McCormick (1809–1884), Joseph Saxton (1799–1873), Charles Goodyear (1800–1860), Peter Cooper (1791–1883), Jordan L. Mott (1799–1866), Joseph Henry (1797–1878), Eliphalet Nott (1773–1866), John Ericsson (1803–1889), Frederick E. Sickels (1818–1895), Samuel F. B. Morse (1791–1872), Henry Burden (1791–1871), Richard Hoe (1815–1884), Erastus B. Bigelow (1814–1879), Isaiah Jennings (1792–1862), Thomas Blanchard (1788–1864), Elias Howe (1819–1867)

———

Christian Schussele (1824–1879)
Oil on canvas, 128.3 × 190.5 cm (50½ × 75 in.), 1862
Gift of the A. W. Mellon Educational and Charitable Trust
NPG.65.60

In the spring of 1861, Ulysses S. Grant hardly seemed destined for greatness. Having resigned his army captain's commission in 1854, this West Point graduate was eking out a living as a clerk. But the Civil War marked a dramatic shift in his fortunes. Reenlisting in the army, he was soon made a general. By war's end, he was commander of all Union land forces and, as the chief architect of the South's defeat, had become one of the country's heroes.

Grant's popularity led to his election to the presidency in 1868, but his weak control over his administration spawned an outbreak of federal corruption that made "Grantism" synonymous with public graft. Nevertheless, his charisma persisted through his two terms.

Mathew Brady photographed General Grant at City Point, Virginia, in 1864. On June 19, Grant reported to his wife, "Brady is along with the Army and is taking a great many views and will send you a copy of each." FSV

Ulysses S. Grant (1822–1885)

———

Mathew Brady (c. 1823–1896)
Albumen silver print, 11.6 × 12.1 cm (4 9/16 × 4 3/4 in.), 1864
In memory of Kenneth G. Murphy
NPG.77.56

In 1843 ex-slave Isabella Van Wagener obeyed God's personal command to her, changed her name to Sojourner Truth, and became an itinerant preacher. Quickly becoming a major attraction on the revival circuit for the power and ingenuity of her prophetic speeches, she was drawn into abolitionism and entranced antislavery audiences with her personal testimony. Like Frederick Douglass (see p. 60), Truth was a charismatic figure because she was not a victim but a leader. She was also a powerful example of African American womanhood. As she concluded in a compelling oration on women's rights, "I could work as much…and bear the lash as well [as a man]! And ain't I a woman?" DCW

Sojourner Truth (c. 1797–1883)

———————

Unidentified photographer
Albumen silver print, 8.1 × 5.7 cm (3³⁄₁₆ × 2¼ in.), 1864
NPG.78.207

I SELL THE SHADOW TO SUPPORT THE
SUBSTANCE.
SOJOURNER TRUTH.

Robert E. Lee was born into a family prominent in Virginia society and politics. A young man with an intense desire to prove himself, he attained the highest rank available to cadets at West Point and graduated from West Point in 1829.

Initially, Lee opposed both secession and war. But when Virginia voted to secede from the Union, he resigned from the U.S. Army and went to his native state's defense. Placed in command of the Army of Northern Virginia in June 1862, Lee gave the Confederacy moments of hope with several early victories. By 1864, however, time and resources were working against him, and in May, Ulysses S. Grant (see p. 82) became his last and fateful adversary.

This is one of six photographs that Mathew Brady took of Lee upon his return to his home in Richmond. The date was April 16, 1865, a week after Lee had surrendered to Grant at Appomattox. JGB

Robert E. Lee (1807–1870)

———

Mathew Brady (c. 1823–1896)
Albumen silver print, 20.8 × 15.2 cm (8¾₆ × 6 in.), 1865
NPG.78.243

Today Abraham Lincoln is universally regarded as one of our greatest presidents. Yet from the start of his administration, he was beset with criticism from all sides as he strove to guide the nation in a time of civil war. Over the course of the agonizing conflict, Lincoln's eloquent articulation of the nation's ideals and his eventual call for an end to slavery gradually invested him with grandeur. Following his assassination in April 1865—just days after Robert E. Lee's surrender—that grandeur became unassailable.

One of the most haunting images in American history and art, this portrait was made in February 1865. The image it presents of Lincoln—hollowed and careworn, yet with a slight smile even after four years of war—takes on added poignancy with the crack that formed in the glass negative after it was developed. Though inadvertent, the crack seems to evoke the division of the Union that Lincoln dedicated himself to mending. With his death, cracks would again appear in that Union as the nation struggled to reconstruct its deeply divided states into a reunified whole. DCW/AMS

Abraham Lincoln (1809–1865)

———

Alexander Gardner (1821–1882)
Albumen silver print, 45 × 38.6 cm (17¹¹⁄₁₆ × 15³⁄₁₆ in.), 1865
NPG.81.M1

An actor turned inventor, Isaac Singer democratized clothing production with the sewing machine he patented in 1851. Although not the first (Elias Howe—see p. 80—introduced a design in 1846), Singer's machine was more reliable and capable of continuous stitching. Hailed two years after its appearance as "one of the most efficient labor-saving devices ever introduced to public notice," Singer's machine could sew nine hundred stitches per minute, more than twenty times as many as a skilled seamstress. Aiming the product at women and putting it within reach of a wide range of buyers, Singer and his business partner Edward Clark established an international commercial empire.

Singer commissioned this portrait while living in Paris, after scandals about his private life forced him to relocate to Europe. English artist Edward Harrison May painted him in clothing that reflects his wealth and trademark extravagance. ACG

Isaac Singer (1811–1875)

————

Edward Harrison May (1824–1887)
Oil on canvas, 130.8 × 98.7 cm (51½ × 38⅞ in.), 1869
Gift of the Singer Company
NPG.75.37

Before embarking on her celebrated writing career, Edith Newbold Jones Wharton led a privileged life as a member of New York society. Edward Harrison May, a British-born artist working in Paris, painted her portrait during an extensive family sojourn in Europe. Wharton, who would become famous for her critical depictions of the New York upper class, as in the Pulitzer Prize–winning *Age of Innocence* (1920), was strongly influenced by these European trips of her youth. As an adult she chose to spend much of her life abroad, forming friendships with other American expatriates, such as Henry James. Despite Wharton's cheerful demeanor in this portrait, she would later chronicle the frustrations of her childhood. Still, it was during this time that she came to enjoy "making up," occupying the fictional worlds she would write about as an adult. ACG

Edith Wharton (1862–1937)

———

Edward Harrison May (1824–1887)
Oil on canvas, 73 × 60.3 cm (28 ¾ × 23 ¾ in.), 1870
NPG.82.136

James McNeill Whistler

An innovative painter, designer, and printmaker, James McNeill Whistler frequently identified his landscapes and portraits as "symphonies," "nocturnes," and "arrangements," demonstrating his interest in atmosphere, color, and line. Although often neglected in his native United States, Whistler was lionized by the avant-garde of Europe, and his most productive years were spent in London and Paris. A self-conscious dandy and aesthete, he possessed a barbed wit and love of affectation that only heightened his celebrity. Commenting on his birthplace in Lowell, Massachusetts, Whistler once declared, "I shall be born when and where I want, and I do not choose to be born at Lowell."

Joseph Edgar Boehm sculpted this bust in 1872, the year in which Whistler exhibited his now-famous *Arrangement in Grey and Black: Portrait of the Artist's Mother* at the Royal Academy in London. ACG

James McNeill Whistler (1834–1903)

———

Joseph Edgar Boehm (1834–1890)
Terra-cotta, 68.6 cm (27 in.) height, 1872
Bequest of Albert E. Gallatin
NPG.65.74

The American impressionist Mary Cassatt spent her career in Europe, settling in Paris. Stifled by tradition, she regarded her exposure to the work of Edgar Degas in 1874 as a "turning point in my artistic life." After her rejection by the Paris Salon of 1877, Cassatt welcomed Degas's invitation to exhibit with the impressionists in 1879.

Cassatt and Degas engaged in lively dialogues about the depiction of modern life, and their vibrant artistic exchange is evident in her willingness to model for him on several occasions. They also collected each other's work. Degas captures the collaborative nature of their friendship in this portrait, where Cassatt is shown in what may be a photography studio holding photographs, possibly reproductions of works of art, seated, as if in the midst of conversation. DDM

Mary Cassatt (1844–1926)

———————

Edgar Degas (1834–1917)
Oil on canvas, 73.3 × 60 cm (28 ⅞ × 23 ⅝ in.), c. 1880–84
Gift of The Morris and Gwendolyn Cafritz Foundation and the
Regents' Major Acquisitions Fund, Smithsonian Institution
NPG.84.34

Born in a log cabin on the Ohio frontier, Annie Oakley earned international fame as an extraordinary markswoman. At the age of nine, she discovered her talent for shooting with hairsplitting accuracy when she began hunting wild game to help feed her siblings and widowed mother. At sixteen, Oakley won a shooting contest in Cincinnati, besting the vaudeville favorite, Frank E. Butler. The two would later marry, and in 1885 they joined Buffalo Bill's Wild West show (see p. 114). For the next seventeen years, Oakley was the show's star attraction. Her shooting feats were unmatched and included hitting a dime tossed in midair at ninety feet. A role model who championed women's participation in area sports, Oakley was also widely admired for her philanthropy.

Declaring it "impossible to shoot brilliantly in a tight-fitting bodice—absolutely impossible," Oakley performed in feminine costumes of her own design that allowed her to move freely and shoot straight. AMS

Annie Oakley (1860–1926)

———

John Wood (active 1865–90)
Albumen silver print, 14.2 × 10.2 cm (5⁹⁄₁₆ × 4 in.), c. 1885
Acquired through the generosity of Friends of the Department of Photographs
NPG.2007.190

Trained in Paris at the École des Beaux-Arts, Henry Hobson Richardson became America's leading architect in the late 1800s. He designed a wide range of structures, including churches, railroad stations, department stores, courthouses, libraries, and private homes. Best-known today for Trinity Church in Boston, Massachusetts, Richardson fused the Romanesque style of medieval France with the picturesque style popular in England and the United States.

In this portrait, British artist Hubert von Herkomer found his sitter's girth, accentuated by the rounded pitcher in the background, an ideal metaphor for his character. During the sittings, Herkomer noted that Richardson was "as solid in his friendship as in his figure. Big-bodied, big-hearted, large-minded, full-brained, loving as he is pugnacious." An admirer of Herkomer's work, Richardson created plans for the artist's country house as payment for the likeness. ACG

H. H. Richardson (1838–1886)

———

Hubert von Herkomer (1849–1914)
Oil on canvas, 113 × 142.9 cm (44 ½ × 56 ¼ in.), 1886
NPG.2010.13

Elegantly depicted by British artist Edward Hughes, Juliette Gordon Low radiates the luxury of her elite American birth and marriage to a wealthy Englishman. Low's satisfaction with her privileged lifestyle, however, soon faded. Following her unfaithful husband's death, she became interested in the Girl Guides, an organization established by her friend, British general Sir Robert Baden-Powell, who had also founded the Boy Scouts. Working with disadvantaged girls living near her Scottish estate, Low became a troop leader, imparting practical skills to her charges. After creating troops in London, Low brought the idea to the United States, establishing a troop in her hometown of Savannah, Georgia. In 1915, Low incorporated the Girl Scouts of America. Today the organization continues to inspire girls to pursue "the highest ideals of character, conduct, patriotism, and service that they may become happy and resourceful citizens." ACG

Juliette Gordon Low (1860–1927)

———

Edward Robert Hughes (1832–1908)
Oil on canvas, 133.4 × 96.5 cm (52 ½ × 38 in.), 1887
Gift of the Girl Scouts of the United States of America
NPG.73.5

Ralph Waldo Emerson wrote in 1844 that America had not found a poet worthy of the county's "ample geography" and "incomparable materials." But on July 4, 1855, Walt Whitman published *Leaves of Grass*, announcing himself as that writer. "I am the poet of the body/And I am the poet of the soul," he told Americans, proclaiming that he would encompass all of American nature and democracy by his celebration of the individual.

Whitman did not just celebrate; he created a new art form, structuring his ecstatic poems in long overspilling lines to create a poetry that captured the expansiveness and vitality of America and its people. His romantic modernism created a means of self-expression that has influenced generations of artists, writers, and musicians.

Whitman admired the effect of this photograph by George Cox, calling it *The Laughing Philosopher*. He sent a copy to Alfred, Lord Tennyson, poet laureate of England, who responded that he "liked it much—oh! so much." DCW

Walt Whitman (1819–1892)

———

George C. Cox (1851–1902)
Platinum print, 22.1 × 18.4 cm (8¹¹⁄₁₆ × 7¼ in.), 1887
Gift of Mr. and Mrs. Charles Feinberg
NPG.76.98

Walt Whitman
Sept: '87

Painted during Thomas Edison's visit to Paris for the Universal Exposition of 1889, Abraham A. Anderson's portrait depicts the wealthy entrepreneur at the height of his career. World-renowned for his inventions—including the phonograph, incandescent lamp, and movie camera—Edison, who received numerous honors in Europe, presided over one of the most popular exhibitions at the exposition. Particularly intriguing to audiences was Edison's phonograph, the recent improvement of which Anderson chose to picture. Although Edison patented the device in 1877, earning himself the title of the "Wizard of Menlo Park," eleven years passed before he achieved sufficient clarity of sound to make it commercially viable. Using the word *specie* as a test, Edison labored until it could be properly transmitted. "When that was done," Edison reported, "I knew everything else could be done, which was a fact." ACG

Thomas Edison (1847–1931)

————

Abraham A. Anderson (1847–1940)
Oil on canvas, 114.3 × 138.7 cm (45 × 54⅝ in.), 1890
Gift of Eleanor A. Campbell
NPG.65.23

Louisa May Alcott began to write professionally in her teens when her father, utopian theorist Amos Bronson Alcott, left the family in dire financial straits. She published her first book, *Flower Fables*, in 1854. After serving as a nurse during the Civil War, she produced the memoir *Hospital Sketches* in 1863. Asked by her publisher to write a book for girls, Alcott drew upon her own family experiences to write *Little Women* (1868). This heartwarming novel, chronicling the lives of the four March sisters—Meg, Jo, Beth, and Amy—was a success at its publication and remains an American literary classic. AEH

Louisa May Alcott (1832–1888)

———

Frank Edwin Elwell (1858–1922)
Bronze, 72.4 cm (28 ½ in.) height, 1967 cast after 1891 plaster
Gift in memory of Alcott Farrar Elwell (1886–1962) by his wife,
Helen Chaffee Elwell
NPG.68.5

For nearly four decades, journalist, editor, and activist Ida B. Wells-Barnett waged a fearless campaign to end the scourge of lynching in America. The daughter of former slaves, Wells mounted a challenge to racial inequality in 1883 when she sued the railroad after being dragged from her seat for refusing to move to a segregated car. She began contributing articles to black-owned newspapers and became part owner and editor of the *Memphis Free Speech and Headlight* in 1889. When three black businessmen were lynched in Memphis in 1892, Wells launched her anti-lynching crusade by investigating other lynchings and publishing her landmark treatise *Southern Horrors: Lynch Law in All Its Phases*. After marrying Chicago lawyer Ferdinand Barnett in 1895, Wells-Barnett continued her activism by founding anti-lynching societies and African American women's clubs, and joining W. E. B. Du Bois to oppose those who advocated gradualism and accommodation in the quest for social equality. AMS

Ida B. Wells-Barnett (1862–1931)

———

Mary Garrity (active 1890s)
Albumen silver print, 13.9 × 9.8 cm (5½ × 3⅞ in.), c. 1893
NPG.2009.36

1843

MISS GARRITY.

PHOTOGRAPHER.

CHICAGO.

Loïe Fuller burst onto Paris's theatrical scene in 1893 with her groundbreaking serpentine dance. Born Marie Louise Fuller in a suburb of Chicago, she began to perform on stage as a child, gaining some success in her teenage years as an actress, singer, dancer, and temperance lecturer. Her career took off when she created a dance that combined the grace of ballet with the technical innovation of electric lighting. The swirling fabrics and bright colors of her performance appealed to the young artists of her adopted country.

Fuller chose Jules Chéret to create this poster advertising her sensationally popular appearances at the Folies-Bergère. A pioneer of the color lithographic poster, Chéret was known for his brilliant hues, described by one critic as "a hooray of reds, a hallelujah of yellows, and a primal scream of blues." His rendition of Fuller inspired other artists to follow suit. ACG

Loïe Fuller (1862–1928)

———

Jules Chéret (1836–1932)
Color lithographic poster, 130.2 × 91.9 cm (51¼ × 36³⁄₁₆ in.), 1893
NPG.84.109

William F. "Buffalo Bill" Cody arguably did more than any single American to popularize the myth of the American West. Before achieving international fame as a showman, he worked a variety of short-term jobs, including Pony Express rider, army scout, and hunting guide. Nicknamed "Buffalo Bill" because of his prowess in hunting buffalo, Cody entered the world of entertainment after a dime novelist in New York wrote a story about his exploits in the West. A subsequent offer to appear on stage led first to a theatrical career and ultimately to the creation of Buffalo Bill's Wild West show in 1882. For the next thirty years, he was the centerpiece of this wildly popular touring display that combined rodeo and historical reenactment. Colorful posters such as this did much to advertise his show and to enhance his larger-than-life reputation. FHG

Buffalo Bill Cody (1846–1917)

————

Courier Lithography Company (active c. 1882–1905)
Color lithographic poster, 76.2 × 110.8 cm (30 × 43⅝ in.), 1900
NPG.87.55

Like fellow industrialist Andrew Carnegie, Henry Clay Frick grew up in a family of limited means. Yet by age thirty he had made his first million dollars and had positioned himself as a key player in America's industrial development. Believing that steel would be the principal building material of the future, Frick amassed his fortune first by supplying coke—fuel made from coal—to the steel industry and later by partnering with Carnegie to create the world's largest steel company. A cutthroat businessman who opposed labor unions, Frick was aggressive in making his operations more efficient. In 1892, during a violent confrontation with striking steelworkers in Homestead, Pennsylvania, he did not hesitate to call in guards from the Pinkerton Detective Agency and the state militia to break the union's resolve. This double portrait shows the industrialist with his daughter, Helen. FHG

Henry Clay Frick (1849–1919)
Helen Clay Frick (1888–1984)

———

Edmund C. Tarbell (1862–1938)
Oil on canvas, 78.7 × 59.1 cm (31 × 23¼ in.), c. 1910
NPG.81.121

This German poster portrays Jack Johnson, the first black world heavyweight boxing champion, as a dignified athlete of magnificent physique. Advertising a film of his 1910 fight with Jim Jeffries, the image avoids the controversies the bout caused in the United States. Social reformers, who viewed the sport as barbaric, were successful in moving the event from San Francisco to Reno. The match, pitting the "Negroes' Deliverer" against the "Hope of the White Race," also engendered bitter racial overtones. Upsetting notions of white racial superiority, Johnson's decisive victory caused race riots around the country, and the film was banned in many American cities. Without reference to such tensions, the poster, produced by a Hamburg company known for its circus advertising, heralds the emergence of sporting events as a major entertainment industry in twentieth-century global culture. WWR

Jack Johnson (1878–1946)

———

Adolph Friedländer Lithography Company (active 1872–1938)
Color lithographic poster, 85.7 × 57.8 cm (33¾ × 22¾ in.), c. 1910
NPG.89.27

Using the pen name Mark Twain, Samuel Clemens had become one of this country's favorite satiric writers by the early 1870s, routinely making light of everyday human foibles. But it was the publication of *The Adventures of Tom Sawyer* (1876) and *The Adventures of Huckleberry Finn* (1884) that assured him a lasting place in American letters. Inspired in part by his own boyhood, these two tales set along the Mississippi River did more than capture the rhythms of youth in antebellum America. In both novels, Clemens examined with sardonic wit various tensions that underlay contemporary society, including, most important, the question of race. In later years, his success in this country and abroad was tempered by financial and personal setbacks and by contempt for American and British imperialism. FHG

Samuel L. Clemens (1835–1910)

———

John White Alexander (1856–1915)
Oil on canvas, 192.4 × 92.1 cm (75¾ × 36¼ in.), c. 1912
NPG.81.116

One of the most successful African American entrepreneurs of the early twentieth century, Madam C. J. Walker created a line of phenomenally popular hair-care and beauty products that fueled a business empire. In 1905, after devising a restorative formula used in combination with her improved steel hot comb to treat thinning and damaged hair, she began marketing her products and beauty regimen to the black community. During a troubled period in the history of race relations in America, Walker built a lucrative enterprise that employed thousands who served as her agents or manufactured her beauty aids. By the time of her death, she was reputed to be the first female African American millionaire.

This portrait by famed African American photographer Addison N. Scurlock became Walker's trademark image. It was featured on packaging for her products and used extensively in her advertising. AMS

Madam C. J. Walker (1867–1919)

———

Addison N. Scurlock (1883–1964)
Gelatin silver print, 13.1 × 8.8 cm (5³⁄₁₆ × 3⁷⁄₁₆ in.), c. 1914
Gift of A'Lelia Bundles and the Walker Family
NPG.2008.20

A celebrated warrior as a young man, Plenty Coups played a crucial role in leading the Crow Indians during the difficult transition to reservation life. Not unlike his near contemporary Booker T. Washington, he stressed the importance of education as a means to maintain tribal integrity and urged his people to become self-sufficient farmers. Although Plenty Coups became a Catholic, he revered and sought to carry on the Crows' native religion and traditional folkways. Dressed in ceremonial regalia, Plenty Coups is thought to have posed for this photograph at the outset of his 1921 trip to Washington, D.C., where he served as the Native American representative at the burial of the unknown soldier of World War I at Arlington National Cemetery. Three years later, in part because of the Native American contribution to World War I, the landmark Indian Citizenship Act was passed. FHG

Plenty Coups (c. 1848–1932)

————

Willem Wildschut (1883–1955)
Gelatin silver print, 91.4 × 61 cm (36 × 24 in.), c. 1921
Gift of the Ruth and Vernon Taylor Foundation,
Beatrice and James Taylor
NPG.2004.128

American expatriate writer Gertrude Stein was a high priestess of early-twentieth-century modernism for the many who visited her fabled Paris apartment. She collected and promoted the art of the avant-garde, including that of Pablo Picasso and Henri Matisse; her own abstract, repetitive prose inspired the experiments of playwrights, composers, poets, and painters. "There was an eternal quality about her," sculptor Jo Davidson wrote. "She somehow symbolized wisdom." He chose to depict her here as "a sort of modern Buddha." Delighted by the sculpture, Stein composed one of her famous prose portraits of Davidson, later published in *Vanity Fair* alongside a photograph of this work. WWR

Gertrude Stein (1874–1946)

————

Jo Davidson (1883–1952)
Terra-cotta, 76.2 cm (30 in.) height, 1922–23
Gift of Dr. Maury Leibovitz
NPG.78.196

In the early years of his career, Thomas Hart Benton was among the young painters drawn to abstraction. He soon rejected that brand of modernism, however, and emerged in the 1920s as a leader of the regionalist school of realism, whose primary concern was the portrayal of local life and history in America. Best-known for his panoramic murals, Benton brought to his works a boldness of composition that led one critic to describe him as "the most… vigorous and virile of our painters." Benton made this portrait of himself and his wife, *Self-Portrait with Rita*, at Martha's Vineyard in Massachusetts during the early years of their marriage. In the course of their residence there, he later recalled, "I really began to mature my painting," and the monumentality of this painting's muscular figures anticipates his later work. **WWR**

Thomas Hart Benton (1889–1975)
Rita Piacenza Benton (1896–1975)

———

Self-portrait
Oil on canvas, 124.5 × 100 cm (49 × 39⅜ in.), c. 1924
Gift of Mr. and Mrs. Jack H. Mooney
NPG.75.30

Langston Hughes published his first poem before he left high school, and in 1926, at the age of twenty-four, he achieved national prominence with the publication of his first volume of verse, *The Weary Blues*. Hughes was one of the most prolific and versatile writers of the 1920s Harlem Renaissance, a movement that recognized and celebrated the creative efforts of black artists, singers, composers, and writers. He was sometimes faulted for dwelling on the negative aspects of the African American experience in his poems, short stories, and novels. But even though his work reflected his radical agenda for change, it also radiated a transcendent pride in his heritage.

The German-born artist Winold Reiss, who did a series of large pastels of famous black intellectuals and artists of the era, suggested Hughes's introspective imagination through the pose and background of this portrait. FSV/WWR

Langston Hughes (1902–1967)

———

Winold Reiss (1886–1953)
Pastel on illustration board, 76.3 × 54.9 cm (30¹⁄₁₆ × 21⅝ in.), 1925
Gift of W. Tjark Reiss, in memory of his father, Winold Reiss
NPG.72.82

WINOLD
REISS

Author of more than a dozen volumes of verse, Marianne Moore received virtually every major literary award—including the Pulitzer Prize and the National Book Award—that the United States had to offer. Moore was acclaimed by her contemporaries, including T. S. Eliot, who cited the "original sensibility and alert intelligence" of her poetry. Using unconventional metrical schemes and focusing on such no-nonsense virtues as courage, loyalty, and patience, her innovative and exquisitely crafted verse secured her a leading position among modernist writers.

This portrait by Marguerite Zorach—*Marianne Moore and Her Mother*—evocative of the bright fauvist colors and faceted cubist planes that the artist picked up from four years in Paris, records Moore at an important moment in her rise to fame. It suggests the influence of Moore's mother, who lived with her daughter and edited her poetry, as well as the red-haired dynamism of Moore herself. WWR

Marianne Moore (1887–1972)

—————

Marguerite Zorach (1887–1968)
Oil on canvas, 102.2 × 77.5 cm (40¼ × 30½ in.), 1925
NPG.87.217

Already well-established as musical theater's "fleetest of jazz steppers," Fred Astaire was starring on Broadway in *Funny Face* when he posed for this image. The dancer-actor would achieve his greatest fame in the 1930s, when he went to Hollywood to make movie musicals and teamed up with Ginger Rogers. Starring together in such confections as *The Gay Divorcee*, *Top Hat*, and *Shall We Dance*, Astaire and Rogers brought a romantic glamour to their films that was uniquely their own. Their silver-screen elegance provided moviegoers with a much-welcomed escape from the gray realities of the Great Depression. Astaire had a genius for making his dancing seem effortless, but behind the finished performance, he said, were long days of experimenting that often produced "nothing but exhaustion."

By transforming Astaire's signature top hat into a recurring motif, Edward Steichen offers a clever visual reference to his subject's style and sophistication. AMS

Fred Astaire (1899–1987)

———————

Edward Steichen (1879–1973)
Gelatin silver print, 24.2 × 19.3 cm (9½ × 7⅝ in.), 1927
Acquired in memory of Agnes and Eugene Meyer through the generosity of Katharine Graham and the New York Community Trust, The Island Fund
NPG.2001.15

On May 20, 1927, Charles Lindbergh took off from New York in his single-engine plane, *Spirit of St. Louis*. Thirty-six hours later he landed in Paris, where he was greeted by a hundred thousand wildly cheering French citizens. The shy Lindbergh brought letters of introduction to claim his prize for the first solo nonstop transatlantic flight. His instant fame in Europe grew into tumultuous celebrations in the United States, where millions cheered him and he was awarded the Congressional Medal of Honor. So began America's infatuation with "Lucky Lindy." Later, in the dark days before World War II, Lindbergh's admiration for German efficiency and industry, and his campaign against America's entry into the war, could not fully dim his luster. The "Lone Eagle's" battle with the elements and the machine struck a chord in America's psyche that still reverberates today. SH

Charles Lindbergh (1902–1974)

————

Unidentified photographer
Gelatin silver print, 23.3 × 18.5 cm (9³⁄₁₆ × 7⁵⁄₁₆ in.), 1927
NPG.80.243

Paul Robeson's appearance as *The Emperor Jones* catapulted him to stardom in 1925, and his popularity soared with a 1930 *Othello* that ran for nearly three hundred performances. He is perhaps best known, however, for his portrayal of Joe in both the stage and movie versions of *Show Boat*, singing "Ol' Man River." He stopped making films in 1942, explaining, "The industry is not prepared to permit me to portray the life or express the living interests, hopes, and aspirations of the struggling people from whom I come." Robeson's left-wing sentiments became a focal point of anti-Communism in the postwar era, and his American career largely came to an end. He lived abroad, returning to the United States for a farewell concert at Carnegie Hall in 1958; he lived his later years in seclusion in Philadelphia.

In the late 1920s, the young African American photographer James L. Allen became the portraitist of choice for the principal figures of the Harlem Renaissance. **AEH**

Paul Robeson (1898–1976)

———

James Latimer Allen (1907–1977)
Gelatin silver print, 23.9 × 19.1 cm (9⁷⁄₁₆ × 7½ in.), 1927
NPG.2001.51

Signed by the Boston Red Sox in 1914, the muscular, six-foot–two-inch, 185-pound George Herman "Babe" Ruth was a gifted pitcher who helped the Sox win championships, but in 1919 he shifted to the outfield to utilize his even more impressive skills as a fielder and batter. The next year, the Yankees paid the Sox $125,000 for Ruth, an enormous sum for the time. In his first year as a Yankee, Ruth hit an astonishing fifty-four home runs, more than any *team* in the American League. In 1923—the first season played in Yankee Stadium ("The House That Ruth Built")—he had what he regarded as his best year and led the Yankees to their first of many World Series victories with three homers and a .368 batting average. Ruth's home-run records have been eclipsed, but many view him as the greatest ever to play the game. SH

Babe Ruth (1895–1948)

———————

Nickolas Muray (1892–1965)
Gelatin silver print, 24.5 × 19.5 cm (9⅝ × 7¹¹⁄₁₆ in.), 1927 (printed 1978)
NPG.78.150

In 1954, when Ernest Hemingway received the Nobel Prize for Literature, the committee cited his "mastery of the art of modern narration." In fact, in his short stories and such novels as *The Sun Also Rises* (1926) and *For Whom the Bell Tolls* (1940), Hemingway had in large measure invented a new literary style as he chronicled the disillusionment of a post–World War I "Lost Generation." His terse, powerful prose became a major influence on American literature. Hemingway's own experiences—reporting foreign wars, living the bohemian life in Paris, and adventuring in Africa, Spain, or Cuba—fueled his imagination and helped create his larger-than-life persona. Man Ray's 1928 photograph of a bandaged Hemingway, made after an accident with an overhead window, occasioned the quip from poet Ezra Pound: "How the hellsufferin tomcats did you git drunk enough to fall upwards through the blithering skylight!" WWR

Ernest Hemingway (1899–1961)

⸻

Man Ray (1890–1976)
Gelatin silver print, 22.5 × 17.5 cm (8⅞ × 6⅞ in.), 1928
NPG.77.130

German-born artist Winold Reiss challenged the racial typing of minorities by portraying his African American, Native American, and Asian subjects as dignified individuals. His portrait of sculptor Isamu Noguchi defied the "yellow peril" stereotyping that followed the 1924 National Origins Act banning Chinese and Japanese immigration. With his frontal pose and bold, confrontational gaze, Noguchi, whose father was Japanese, appears as a self-assured, thoroughly modern young American. The abstract background hints at that mix of the organic and geometric that characterized Noguchi's sculpture. At the time, Noguchi had just returned from Paris on a Guggenheim Fellowship. In his grant application, he had stated how he planned to reconcile his dual ethnicity through art: "My father…has long been known as an interpreter of the East to the West, through poetry. I wish to do the same with sculpture." WWR

Isamu Noguchi (1904–1988)

———————

Winold Reiss (1886–1953)
Pastel on paper, 73.7 × 54.6 cm (29 × 21½ in.), c. 1929
Gift of Joseph and Rosalyn Newman
NPG.86.226

During the 1920s and 1930s, the glamorous husband-and-wife team of Ely and Josephine Culbertson succeeded in transforming bridge from a parlor game into an international phenomenon. Already accomplished players when they married in 1923, the duo enjoyed spectacular success on the tournament circuit with their unconventional bidding methods and playing strategies that Ely had pioneered. When contract bridge was introduced in 1926, Ely seized the opportunity to establish himself as the new game's foremost expert and practitioner. After launching *The Bridge World* magazine in 1929 and publishing his best-selling *Contract Bridge Blue Book* the following year, Culbertson partnered with his wife to score victories in a series of high-profile matches at home and abroad. The unprecedented media coverage of these contests made the Culbertsons international celebrities and ignited a contract bridge craze that remained unabated for more than a decade. AMS

Ely Culbertson (1891–1955)
Josephine Dillon Culbertson (1898–1956)

————

Nikol Schattenstein (1877–1954)
Oil on canvas, 127 × 102.3 cm (50 × 40¼ in.), c. 1930
NPG.90.42

In the long struggle for civil rights and racial equality in America, few episodes had the impact of the infamous Scottsboro Boys case. When nine black teenagers falsely accused of raping two women on a freight train were tried in Scottsboro, Alabama, in 1931, white juries found eight of the nine guilty and sentenced them to death. The widely condemned verdicts and the subsequent reversals, retrials, and hearings mobilized protests across the country and around the world.

In this pastel, Aaron Douglas, the leading visual artist of the Harlem Renaissance, portrayed Clarence Norris (left) and Haywood Patterson, whose convictions had been unanimously overturned by the U.S. Supreme Court because of Alabama's exclusion of blacks from the jury rolls. Focusing on the essential humanity and dignity of the subjects, Douglas's moving portrait suggests his profound response to this soul-chilling miscarriage of justice. WWR

The Scottsboro Boys
Clarence Norris (1912–1989)
Haywood Patterson (1913–1952)

———

Aaron Douglas (1899–1979)
Pastel on paper, 41 × 37.1 cm (16⅛ × 14⅝ in.), c. 1935
NPG.2004.6

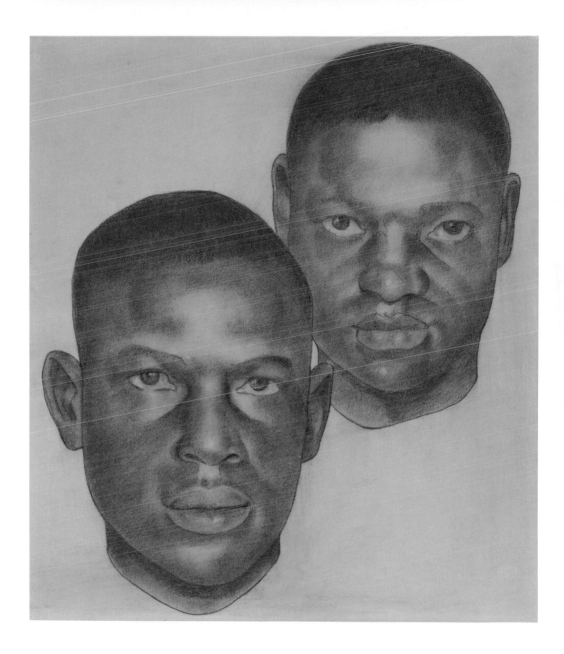

John Steinbeck

In politics, mention of the Great Depression evokes Franklin Roosevelt's New Deal; in painting, it summons up images of federally funded WPA murals depicting the nation's workforce. And in American letters, the work most synonymous with those hard times is *The Grapes of Wrath*, John Steinbeck's best-selling novel portraying the spirit-breaking poverty that overtook so much of the country's rural economy in the wake of prolonged drought and falling crop prices. When the book appeared in 1939, Steinbeck had already tasted popular success with his two novels *Tortilla Flat* (1935) and *Of Mice and Men* (1937). *The Grapes of Wrath*, however, earned him an acclaim that few American writers have enjoyed. No recent novel, one critic said at its publication, was "better calculated to awaken the humanity of others." In 1962, Steinbeck's literary accomplishments earned him the Nobel Prize for Literature. **FSV**

John Steinbeck (1902–1968)

———

Sonya Noskowiak (1900–1975)
Gelatin silver print, 21.7 × 18.4 cm (8⁹⁄₁₆ × 7¼ in.), 1935
NPG.81.14

In the early decades of the twentieth century, when waves of immigration and explosive urban growth transformed the face of America, George Gershwin emerged as a transcendent voice of modernism. His staccato-paced, syncopated rhythms helped define the Jazz Age on Broadway in the 1920s in such shows as *Lady Be Good* and *Girl Crazy*. At the height of the Great Depression, his "folk opera" *Porgy and Bess* attempted to catch the clash and blends of cultural "interfusions" that he saw as distinctively American. And he was part of the Hollywood scene during the golden age of the silver screen, notably completing—with his lyricist brother Ira—the score for *The Goldwyn Follies* just before his death in 1937, at age thirty-nine. Gershwin had become a central force in the lively arts in years marked by a search for a modern American identity. AEH

George Gershwin (1898–1937)

————

Arthur Kaufman (1888–1971)
Oil on canvas, 92.1 × 62.2 cm (36¼ × 24½ in.), 1936
NPG.73.8

By 1937, when Clark Gable and Jean Harlow posed for this promotional picture for their film *Saratoga*, both were at their box office peaks. Harlow established herself as Hollywood's leading sex goddess with her performance in *Hell's Angels* in 1931, but she really came into her own in 1933 with *Bombshell*, in which her brilliant parody of her own reputation as a siren revealed a substantial gift for comedy. One of MGM's top stars, Gable had already won a Best Actor Oscar for *It Happened One Night* (1934), and he would soon be tapped for his most celebrated role, the rakish Rhett Butler in the 1939 screen epic *Gone with the Wind*. Gable and Harlow shared top billing in a number of pictures. Unfortunately, *Saratoga* would be their last co-starring venture. Two months before the picture's release, Harlow died from uremic poisoning. **FSV**

Clark Gable (1901–1960)
Jean Harlow (1911–1937)

————

Clarence Sinclair Bull (1895–1979)
Gelatin silver print, 35.6 × 27.9 cm (14 × 11 in.), 1937
NPG.81.13

Considered the mother of modern dance in America, Martha Graham brought dance into the vortex of the machine age: the idea of motion was a fundamental tenet of modernism, and Graham was determined to extract dance from its balletic— and European—classicism and infuse it with "significant movement…with excitement and surge." She studied at Ruth St. Denis and Ted Shawn's Denishawn School from 1916 to 1923 and then worked at the Greenwich Village Follies, where she began to design and choreograph her own dances. By 1935 she had established the Martha Graham School for Contemporary Dance, and its first performance, "Frontier," reflected her notion that "life today is nervous, sharp, and zigzag." Graham continued to perform until she was seventy-six and created new ballets until her death. AEH

Martha Graham (1894–1991)

⸻

Paul R. Meltsner (1905–1966)
Oil on canvas, 106.7 × 81.3 cm (42 × 32 in.), 1938
NPG.73.41

Will Rogers, who was part Cherokee, once told a Boston audience, "My ancestors didn't come over on the *Mayflower*—they met the boat." He spent his youth in traveling circuses as a rope artist and roughrider, later adding jokes to his lariat tricks. Eventually he wound up on the vaudeville circuit, and by 1912 on Broadway, where he became a star of the Ziegfeld *Follies*. He also embarked on a motion picture and then a radio career that would establish him as America's homespun philosopher. When he died in an airplane crash in 1935, Rogers was arguably the nation's best-loved personality. AEH

Will Rogers (1879–1935)

————

Jo Davidson (1883–1952)
Bronze, 47.6 cm (18¾ in.) height, cast after 1938 original
NPG.67.52

Pictured here with his family, Fred Korematsu fought a lifelong struggle to right an injustice that the U.S. government brought upon thousands of Japanese Americans. Korematsu was a welder on the Oakland docks before the Japanese attack on Pearl Harbor. On February 19, 1942, President Franklin D. Roosevelt (see p. 174) signed an executive order authorizing West Coast military commanders to issue whatever orders they thought were necessary for national security. The relocation of Japanese Americans into internment camps soon followed. Korematsu defied the order, was sent to federal prison, and later joined his family in a detention center. With the aid of the American Civil Liberties Union, he challenged the legality of the detention, but it was upheld by the U. S. Supreme Court in 1944. In 1983 Korematsu petitioned to reopen the case, arguing that the government had known that Japanese Americans were not a security threat. A lower court found in his favor, and his conviction was overturned. In 1988 Congress apologized for the internments and awarded each survivor $20,000. AMS

Fred Korematsu (1919–2005)

————

Unidentified photographer
Gelatin silver print, 12 × 16.9 cm (4¾ × 6⅝ in.), 1939
Gift of the Fred T. Korematsu Family
NPG.2010.118

Helena Rubinstein was a pioneer at a time when it was difficult for women to succeed in the male-dominated business world. She first made her reputation through the specialized treatments she offered to women at her exclusive salons, but she amassed her fortune in the 1920s selling mass-produced cosmetics internationally. Her legendary career paved the way for other entrepreneurial women.

Mexican artist Roberto Montenegro here captures her dynamic personality and dramatic flair. He depicts Rubinstein wearing a specially designed necklace made by William Spratling, who created a center for Mexican jewelry in Taxco during the 1930s. Rubinstein wrote in her autobiography, "Although I no longer need the added courage that handsome jewelry once gave me (it was not easy being a hard-working woman in a man's world many years ago), I am aware that the wearing of exotic jewelry has become…a mark of my identity." DDM

Helena Rubinstein (1870–1965)

————

Roberto Montenegro (1887–1968)
Oil on canvas, 80 × 70.7 cm (31½ × 27¹³⁄₁₆ in.), 1941
NPG.2011.141

Born into slavery, George Washington Carver overcame the obstacles of slender means and racial discrimination to seek an education. He believed that "when you can do the common things of life in an uncommon way, you will command the attention of the world." These words, coupled with his lifelong goal to help poor black farmers trapped in sharecropping and dependency on cotton as a crop, pervaded his work at Alabama's Tuskegee Institute, where he was director of agricultural teaching and research for nearly forty years. Carver's laboratory investigations led to the discovery of more than 450 new commercial products—ranging from margarine to library paste—that could be extracted from previously untapped sources such as the peanut and sweet potato. He demonstrated for southern farmers the wisdom of diversifying crops, instead of relying mainly on the soil-exhausting crop of cotton. FSV

George Washington Carver (1864–1943)

———————

Betsy Graves Reyneau (1888–1964)
Oil on canvas, 114.9 × 89.5 cm (45¼ × 35¼ in.), 1942
Gift of the George Washington Carver Memorial Committee
NPG.65.77

Georgia O'Keeffe's pastel portrait honors Beauford Delaney's perseverance and courage in the face of difficulty. As a gay black painter, Delaney faced many challenges, impeded by sexual, cultural, and racial stereotyping, and eventually beset by psychological problems. Born in Knoxville, Tennessee, Delaney studied in Boston and then settled in New York City before his final migration to Paris. In Greenwich Village and Harlem, Delaney befriended musicians and writers and was introduced to artists, including Georgia O'Keeffe. Although portraiture is rare in her work, O'Keeffe greatly admired Delaney and found him attractive. She rendered her subject in much the same manner as her still lifes of bones, rocks, or flowers. Isolating Delaney's profile against a neutral background, she used minute tonal gradations and beautifully blended pastels to create a powerful, timeless symbol of human endeavor. WWR

Beauford Delaney (1901–1979)

———

Georgia O'Keeffe (1887–1986)
Pastel on paper, 48.9 × 32.4 cm (19¼ × 12¾ in.), 1943
Gift of the Georgia O'Keeffe Foundation
NPG.2002.1

This poster, designed by an Office of War Information art director, David Stone Martin, was one of several inspirational posters aimed at the black community. At the outbreak of World War II, the armed services practiced rigid discrimination against African Americans that included a stubborn reluctance to acknowledge black capabilities. When Japan attacked Pearl Harbor on December 7, 1941, navy messman Dorie Miller was serving on the USS *West Virginia*. Before abandoning ship, he braved enemy fire to carry a wounded officer to safety and, although not trained for combat, manned an antiaircraft gun, possibly downing at least one enemy plane. He eventually received a Navy Cross, but only after intense pressure by the black press. The poster's heroic overtones and quote gain extra poignancy in hindsight: Miller, later a messman on the USS *Liscombe Bay*, was killed when the aircraft carrier sank in the Pacific in November 1943. FSV

Dorie Miller (1919–1943)

———

David Stone Martin (1913–1992)
Color halftone poster, 76.5 × 56.5 cm (30⅛ × 22¼ in.), 1943
NPG.88.173

"above and beyond the call of duty"

DORIE MILLER
Received the Navy Cross
at Pearl Harbor, May 27, 1942

As the nation's first lady, Eleanor Roosevelt rapidly expanded her role from hostess to advocate and emerged as a vital force in her husband Franklin's administration. She took public stands on issues ranging from exploitive labor practices to civil rights, but more important, she often urged her husband toward measures he might otherwise have avoided. When the challenges of World War II drew the president's attention from domestic affairs, she continued to be a strong voice for the New Deal's social welfare policies. The activism that characterized Eleanor Roosevelt's years as first lady did not end with her departure from the White House. As a U.S. delegate to the United Nations (1945–53), she was instrumental in formulating the Universal Declaration of Human Rights and securing its ratification by the General Assembly in 1948.

Eleanor Roosevelt's hands were seldom still, and prominent Canadian photographer Yousuf Karsh captured their expressive qualities in this portrait. AMS

Eleanor Roosevelt (1884–1962)

———

Yousuf Karsh (1908–2002)
Gelatin silver print, 31.5 × 25.5 cm (12⅜ × 10¹⁄₁₆ in.), 1944
Gift of Estrellita Karsh in memory of Yousuf Karsh
NPG.2012.77.89

Nicknamed "Old Blood and Guts," General George Patton had a penchant for harsh, bluntly spoken opinions that sometimes made him the object of controversy during World War II. There was, however, no debating his soldiering abilities. In the Allied drive against Axis armies in North Africa, his gift for instilling frontline discipline was critical in shaping unseasoned American soldiers into effective fighting units. His leadership proved crucial again in the invasion of Sicily, but his finest moment came during the massive German counteroffensive in northern Europe's Ardennes region in 1944–45. His part in repelling the Germans there placed beyond challenge his reputation as one of the most brilliant field commanders of the war.

The inscription in the portrait's upper left corner was from Patton's declaration of May 9, 1945, telling his soldiers what an honor it had been to lead them. FSV

George S. Patton (1885–1945)

———————

Boleslaw Jan Czedekowski (1885–1969)
Oil on canvas, 127 × 103.2 cm (50 × 40⅝ in.), 1945
Gift of Major General George S. Patton, U.S.A., Retired,
and the Patton Family
NPG.99.5

When Franklin Roosevelt began serving in New York's state legis-lature in 1911, some observers declared him ill-suited to the rough realities of politics. But Roosevelt thrived on those realities; some two decades later, he was advancing from the New York governorship to the presidency.

Taking office against the bleak backdrop of the Great Depression, Roosevelt responded quickly to this economic disaster with a host of regulatory and welfare measures that redefined the govern-ment's role in American life. Among conservatives, the new federal involvement in matters traditionally left to the private sector was a betrayal of America's ideals. But in other quarters, Roosevelt's activism inspired an unwavering popularity that led to his election to an unprecedented four terms.

When Roosevelt sat for this portrait in 1945, his presidential concerns had long since shifted to guiding the nation through World War II. This likeness is a study for a larger painting—a sketch of which appears at the lower left—commemorating Roosevelt's meeting at the Yalta Conference with wartime Allied leaders Winston Churchill and Joseph Stalin. **FSV**

Franklin D. Roosevelt (1882–1945)

———

Douglas Chandor (1897–1953)
Oil on canvas, approx. 110.5 × 90.2 cm (43½ × 35½ in.), 1945
NPG.68.49

AD FAMILIAM GENTIVM COMEM CONTENDIT

STUDY OF
PRESIDENT ROOSEVELT
FOR PAINTING
"BIG THREE AT YALTA"
CANVAS SIZE 92" × 92"
WITH OUTLINE SKETCH

CHANDOR MARCH 1945. THE WHITE HOUSE, WASHINGTON.

Leonard Bernstein

Like George Gershwin (see p. 152) before him, Leonard Bernstein exulted in the staccato rhythms of the city—especially New York City. His career flourished on a parallel course as a composer, pianist, and conductor: he was hailed as an overnight sensation in 1943 when he replaced an ailing Bruno Walter as conductor of the New York Philharmonic. Shortly afterward, he met choreographer Jerome Robbins, and they created the ballet *Fancy Free* (1944). Bernstein was intent on composing music with a fast-paced, authentic American voice, and—with his own heyday paralleling the golden age of the American musical—he captured the pulsing energy of the city in his most popular works: *On the Town*, *Wonderful Town*, and *West Side Story*. He also helped popularize music of all kinds in his legendary *Young People's Concerts*, which were broadcast on television to wide audiences beginning in 1958. AEH

Leonard Bernstein (1918–1990)

—————

Irving Penn (1917–2009)
Gelatin silver print, 24.2 × 19.4 cm (9½ × 7⅝ in.), 1947
NPG.90.125

Singer and actress Lena Horne helped break the color barrier in mainstream popular culture in the mid-twentieth century, beginning her stage career in the chorus at Harlem's Cotton Club in 1933, where Duke Ellington and Cab Calloway mentored her. In 1942 Hollywood beckoned, but her roles were often musical cameos that southern theaters could cut; Horne once said that *Stormy Weather* and *Cabin in the Sky* (both 1943) were the only films "in which I played a character who was involved in the plot." She became Hollywood's highest-paid African American actor, and her renditions of the songs "Stormy Weather" and "Just One of Those Things" are considered classics. During this time, Horne also became a vocal spokesperson for civil rights. She also continued to enjoy a successful nightclub and recording career, and triumphed in the 1980s with her one-woman show, *Lena Horne: The Lady and Her Music.* AEH

Lena Horne (1917–2010)

———

Edward Biberman (1904–1986)
Oil on canvas, 129.5 × 78.7 cm (51 × 31 in.), 1947
NPG.85.2

Jackie Robinson

As the first African American to play major league baseball, Jackie Robinson was a pioneer in professional sports. This 1947 photograph by Harry Warnecke pictures Robinson at Ebbets Field during his first season with the Brooklyn Dodgers. That year was both glorious and unnerving. While winning Rookie of the Year honors and helping the Dodgers to win the National League pennant, Robinson faced intense scrutiny. As he later recalled, "I had to fight hard against loneliness, abuse, and the knowledge that any mistake I made would be magnified because I was the only black man out there." Robinson paved the way for black major leaguers such as Willie Mays and Hank Aaron. A lifetime .311 hitter, Robinson led the Dodgers to six pennants and one World Series title during his ten-year career. After retiring from the game, he remained a staunch advocate for civil rights while building a successful business career. FHG/AMS

Jackie Robinson (1919–1972)

———

Harry Warnecke (1900–1984)
Color carbro print, 32.4 × 25.7 cm (12¾ × 10⅛ in.), 1947
NPG.97.219

George C. Marshall was, according to one expert observer, the "perfect" soldier. Endowed with a quick mind, a good memory, and a superb sense of strategy, he did not particularly relish war. Yet as chief of staff during World War II, he proved to be a masterful orchestrator of military mobilization. In 1945 President Harry Truman remarked that millions of Americans had served the country well in that conflict, but it had been Marshall who "gave it victory." As capable in peace as in wartime, Marshall later became Truman's secretary of state, and it was he who unveiled in 1947 the American aid program for rebuilding Europe's war-ravaged economies. Ultimately named the Marshall Plan, this venture became one of the greatest triumphs in the entire history of American diplomacy. FSV

George C. Marshall (1880–1959)

———

Thomas E. Stephens (1886–1966)
Oil on canvas, 127 × 101.5 cm (50 × 39¹⁵⁄₁₆), 1949
Gift of Ailsa Mellon Bruce
NPG.65.66

Jackson Pollock

Jackson Pollock was an explosive force in American art circles at midcentury. Rejecting the realism of his mentor, Thomas Hart Benton (see p. 128), Pollock developed a painting style centered on spontaneity and accident. Rather than working on an easel, he laid his canvases on the studio floor and used a variety of non-traditional tools, including sticks and trowels, to create swirling patterns of expressive paint. Inspired by Jungian psychology and surrealism, he sought an art that flowed with great immediacy from his unconscious. From the time of his first solo exhibition in 1943 to his death in a car accident in 1956, Pollock was the most talked about and controversial artist of the period. His hard drinking, reckless behavior, and brooding manner only added to the public's fascination.

Photographer Hans Namuth captured Pollock's "action painting" in a series of five hundred photographs and two films, revealing his signature pouring technique to the world. **FHG**

Jackson Pollock (1912–1956)

———————

Hans Namuth (1915–1990)
Gelatin silver print, 37.6 × 35.1 cm (14¹³⁄₁₆ × 13¹³⁄₁₆ in.), 1950
Gift of the Estate of Hans Namuth
NPG.95.155

Commander of American land forces in the Pacific at the outbreak of World War II, General Douglas MacArthur suffered the worst defeat of his career in the spring of 1942, when he was forced to flee the Philippines in the wake of Japanese invasion. Uttering on his arrival in Australia his famous words, "I shall return," MacArthur now faced the task of repelling Japan's drive for dominion in the south-west Pacific. His success in that effort, combined with his own genius for self-promotion in the press, made him one of the most popular heroes of the war back in civilian America. By the time he made good his promise to retake the Philippines in spring 1945, his reputation had reached legendary proportions, and the following September he was chosen to preside over Japan's final surrender. FSV

Douglas MacArthur (1880–1964)

———

Howard Chandler Christy (1873–1952)
Oil on canvas, 137.8 × 100.3 cm (54¼ × 39½ in.), c. 1952
Gift of Henry Ostrow
NPG.78.271

When James Dean died in a car crash in 1955, his career as a movie actor had barely begun. The only films to his credit were *East of Eden*, *Rebel without a Cause*, and *Giant*, the last two of which had not even been released. But the tragedy of his untimely death and the combination of youthful rage and sensitivity that he radiated on the screen was enough to inspire a Dean cult among moviegoers that continued for several decades. The admiration for Dean extended to his fellow Hollywood professionals, and his performances in both *East of Eden* and *Giant* earned him posthumous Best Actor nominations from the Motion Picture Academy.

Introduced to Dean through a mutual friend in 1954, Roy Schatt photographed Dean throughout the year and taught him rudimentary camera skills. During their outings, the two often took turns photographing one another. Schatt took this portrait, made with available light, during a visit to Dean's tiny New York apartment. He later called Dean "a paradoxical combination of egomaniac and loner, wanting to be seen yet hiding from the public." FSV/ACG

James Dean (1931–1955)

———

Roy Schatt (1909–2002)
Gelatin silver print, 34.7 × 42.2 cm (13¹¹⁄₁₆ × 16⅝ in.), 1954
Gift of Mr. and Mrs. Roy Schatt
NPG.91.209

In 1942, at government request, physicist J. Robert Oppenheimer began investigating the feasibility of an atomic bomb for the United States. A year later he became director of a laboratory charged with developing this weapon, and on July 16, 1945, he witnessed the explosion of the world's first atomic bomb. At the time, Oppenheimer said, a passage from the Bhagavad-Gita came to mind: "I am become Death, the shatterer of Worlds."

During the Cold War, Oppenheimer became a target of the House Un-American Activities Committee's anti-Communist suspicions. Despite his wide acclaim, Oppenheimer was declared a security risk for his misgivings about the bomb. The cloud of suspicion surrounding him never entirely cleared, and he retired to Princeton University, where he became director of the Institute for Advanced Study.

The accusations leveled at Oppenheimer in the early 1950s won him many sympathizers. Among them was the artist Ben Shahn, who in this drawing gave Oppenheimer the look of a man whose dignity both as a person and a scientist had been wrongfully violated. FSV/WWR

J. Robert Oppenheimer (1904–1967)

———

Ben Shahn (1898–1969)
Ink on paper, 29.7 × 13.3 cm (11¹¹⁄₁₆ × 5¼ in.), 1954
NPG.84.192

Arturo Toscanini said that Marian Anderson had a voice that came along "once in a hundred years." When one of Anderson's teachers first heard her sing, the magnitude of her talent moved him to tears. Because she was black, however, her initial prospects as a concert singer in this country were sharply limited, and her early professional triumphs took place mostly in Europe. The magnitude of her musical gifts ultimately won her recognition in the United States as well. Despite that acclaim, in 1939 the Daughters of the American Revolution banned her from performing at its Constitution Hall. First Lady Eleanor Roosevelt (see p. 170) ultimately intervened and facilitated Anderson's Easter Sunday outdoor concert at the Lincoln Memorial—an event witnessed by seventy-five thousand and broadcast to a radio audience of millions. The affair generated great sympathy for Anderson and became a defining moment in America's civil rights movement. FHG

Marian Anderson (1897–1993)

———

Betsy Graves Reyneau (1888–1964)
Oil on canvas, 153 × 97.5 cm (60¼ × 38⅜ in.), 1955
Gift of the Harmon Foundation
NPG.67.76

Audrey Hepburn's first major motion picture, *Roman Holiday* (1953), won the actress an Academy Award and launched a career that would make her one of the most celebrated movie stars of her generation. Successful films, such as *Sabrina* (1954), *Breakfast at Tiffany's* (1961), and *My Fair Lady* (1964), along with a lifelong friendship and collaboration with designer Hubert de Givenchy, helped to maintain Hepburn's image of elegance and poise.

In this portrait, the newly married actress posed for celebrity photographer Philippe Halsman at her rented villa outside Rome during the shooting of *War and Peace*. A variant of this image appeared on the cover of *Life* magazine in 1955. Halsman captures Hepburn's delicate beauty and impish charm, which won the hearts of audiences everywhere. Late in her life, Hepburn became a goodwill ambassador for UNICEF, committing herself to raising awareness of impoverished children around the globe. ACG

Audrey Hepburn (1929–1993)

———

Philippe Halsman (1906–1979)
Gelatin silver print, 34.9 × 27 cm (13¾ × 10⅝ in.), 1955
NPG.95.96

In the first rank of American composers, Edward Kennedy "Duke" Ellington was—to use a favorite phrase of his own—"beyond category." He produced what has been called the "single most impressive body of composition in American jazz": more than two thousand compositions that ranged from such popular classics as "Satin Doll" and "Sophisticated Lady" to extended works such as *Black, Brown and Beige*, which premiered at Carnegie Hall in 1943. Ellington continually expanded his work as a composer and bandleader, composing for Broadway (*Beggar's Opera*) and Hollywood (including the film score for *Anatomy of a Murder*), undertaking extensive international tours, and working with younger jazz musicians such as John Coltrane, Charles Mingus, and Max Roach. He received the 1965 Pulitzer Prize for his long-term achievement and the Presidential Medal of Freedom in 1969. **AEH**

Duke Ellington (1899–1974)

———————

Peter Hurd (1904–1984)
Tempera on board, 48.3 × 34.3 cm (19 × 13½ in.), 1956
Time cover, August 20, 1956
Gift of *Time* magazine
NPG.78.TC353

Thurgood Marshall was a major figure in the civil rights movement of the mid-twentieth century, first as counsel for the NAACP (1938–61) and then as the first African American justice on the U. S. Supreme Court. Born in Baltimore, Maryland, Marshall went to Howard University Law School, which was pioneering a conception of the law as proactive, especially on issues of race relations. Spearheading the NAACP's challenges to the legal basis for racial discrimination, especially the doctrine of "separate but equal," Marshall's crowning achievement was the unanimous Supreme Court decision *Brown v. Board of Education of Topeka* (1954), which ruled that segregation of public schools by race was unconstitutional. In 1967 President Lyndon Johnson named Marshall to the Supreme Court where, over a career lasting until 1991, he found himself increasingly isolated as the court became more conservative. DCW

Thurgood Marshall (1908–1993)

———

Betsy Graves Reyneau (1888–1964)
Oil on canvas, 127 × 81.3 cm (50 × 32 in.), 1956
Gift of the Harmon Foundation
NPG.67.43

Henri Cartier-Bresson's photograph shows Malcolm X sitting at a restaurant table before a framed poster of Elijah Muhammad. It was Muhammad, head of the black separatist group Nation of Islam, who was most responsible for redirecting the former Malcolm Little from the life of a petty criminal to that of a national civil rights leader.

Malcolm X rose to his position of authority in the early 1960s as an outspoken critic of Martin Luther King Jr. (see p. 206) and others who were, in his words, "begging for integration." The Nation of Islam has "shaken up the white man by asking for separation," he said in 1961. Although Malcolm X would later reject the Nation of Islam and make peace with King, he was instrumental in making the civil rights campaign more militant and in planting the seeds for the Black Power movement. **FHG**

Malcolm X (1925–1965)

———

Henri Cartier-Bresson (1908–2004)
Gelatin silver print, 25 × 16.8 cm (9¹³⁄₁₆ × 6⅝ in.), 1961
NPG.2004.33

Medgar Evers (on right, with sign) played a critical role in organizing and sustaining the Jackson Movement—a multifaceted campaign to end segregation in Mississippi's most populous city. In the spring of 1963, Evers launched a boycott of stores in Jackson's main shopping district after the city's mayor rejected a NAACP-sponsored resolution calling for fair hiring practices in municipal jobs, desegregation of public facilities and accommodations, an end to discriminatory business practices, and the establishment of a biracial committee to combat injustice and promote reform. When NAACP national secretary Roy Wilkins joined Evers in picketing the F. W. Woolworth store in downtown Jackson, both men were swiftly arrested by local police brandishing electric cattle prods. This press photograph documenting the arrest appeared in the *New York Times* on June 2, 1963—just ten days before Evers's assassination by white supremacist Byron de la Beckwith. AMS

Roy Wilkins (1901–1981)
Medgar Evers (1925–1963)

———

Unidentified photographer
Gelatin silver print, 19.4 × 24.2 cm (7⅝ × 9½ in.), 1963
NPG.2001.81

When an assassin's bullet cut short John F. Kennedy's presidency in November 1963, the country experienced a collective sense of loss. But the grief was not so much inspired by Kennedy's presidential accomplishments as it was an expression of what he had come to represent: his eloquence and idealism had made him, in the eyes of many, the embodiment of this country's finest aspirations. Still, his administration could claim triumphs in foreign policy, including a successful face-off with the Soviets over the presence of missiles in Cuba. Its support for the civil rights movement, moreover, would soon give birth to landmark legislation promoting racial equality.

Elaine de Kooning arranged for sittings with Kennedy in late 1962, intending to complete a single portrait. Fascinated with the changeability of Kennedy's features, she instead painted an entire series of likenesses, including this one. In its loose, almost chaotic brushwork, the portrait illustrates de Kooning's close identification with the abstract expressionist movement of the 1950s. FSV

John F. Kennedy (1917–1963)

———

Elaine de Kooning (1918–1989)
Oil on canvas, 260.4 × 111.8 cm (102½ × 44 in.), 1963
NPG.99.75

Martin Luther King Jr.

Under the leadership of Martin Luther King Jr., nonviolent protest became the defining feature of the civil rights movement. A brilliant strategist, King first demonstrated the efficacy of passive resistance in 1955, when he led the prolonged bus boycott in Montgomery, Alabama, that resulted in the dismantling of bus segregation laws. Fresh from a victory that had brought him national recognition, the charismatic young clergyman helped found the Southern Christian Leadership Conference and took the lead in directing its civil rights initiatives. In a carefully orchestrated campaign of peaceful protest to expose and defeat racial injustice, King awakened the nation's conscience and galvanized support for the landmark civil rights legislation of the 1960s. King's words were as powerful as his deeds, and the moving and eloquent addresses that gave hope to millions continue to inspire people throughout the world: "I have a dream that one day this nation will rise up, live out the true meaning of its creed: 'We hold these truths to be self-evident, that all men are created equal.'"

King was assassinated on April 4, 1968, while in Memphis, Tennessee, to support a strike by sanitation workers. AMS

Martin Luther King Jr. (1929–1968)

———

Robert Vickrey (born 1926)
Tempera on paper, approx. 37.5 × 28.5 cm (14¾ × 11¼ in.), 1963
Time cover, January 3, 1964
Gift of *Time* magazine
NPG.78.TC517

Soprano Leontyne Price trained at Juilliard and first scored a major success in 1952, appearing as Bess in a touring production of George Gershwin's *Porgy and Bess*. In 1955 she appeared in an NBC telecast of *Tosca* and was subsequently in high demand by opera houses in London, Vienna, and Milan. It was not until 1961 that she made her debut at the Metropolitan Opera—as Leonora in *Il Trovatore*—and she quickly became a Met favorite until her farewell performance there in 1985. Especially associated with the works of Verdi and Samuel Barber, Price sang the title role in *Cleopatra*—which Barber created for her—at the opening of the Met's new home at Lincoln Center. Price was also a tireless performer on the recital circuit and has won fifteen Grammys for her recordings. AEH

Leontyne Price (born 1927)

———

Bradley Phillips (1929–1991)
Oil on canvas, 127.6 × 92.1 cm (50¼ × 36¼ in.), 1963
Gift of Ms. Sayre Sheldon
NPG.91.96

As a visiting nurse among New York City's immigrants in the early 1900s, Margaret Sanger was profoundly affected by the physical and mental toll exacted on women by frequent childbirth, miscarriage, and self-induced abortion. Faced with laws forbidding dissemination of contraceptive information, Sanger's crusade had much opposition. But by 1921, when Sanger founded the Birth Control League, her movement had begun to win adherents in respectable quarters. Adding to her life of controversy is her association with the eugenics movement—which included promotion of forced sterilization for those deemed mentally unfit—a movement that for a time was endorsed by many of the era's prominent thinkers. SH

Margaret Sanger (1879–1966)

———

Joy Buba (1904–1998)
Bronze, 52.1 cm (20 ½ in.) height, 1972 cast after 1964 original
Gift of Mrs. Cordelia Scaife May
NPG.72.70

As a government scientist, Rachel Carson became concerned about the ecological impact of pesticides, especially DDT, and in 1962 she published the groundbreaking *Silent Spring*. Finely written and passionately reasoned, *Silent Spring* exploded into national consciousness and can be said to have started the modern environmental movement. Although some of its conclusions are still controversial today, the book was a warning that an active citizenry had to be skeptical of large institutions, an attitude that became a dominant theme of the 1960s and 1970s.

Sculptor Una Hanbury, who met Carson shortly before her death, was struck by her tremendous vitality and incorporated that quality into her portrait. WWR/DCW

Rachel Carson (1907–1964)

———

Una Hanbury (1904–1990)
Bronze, 48.6 cm (19⅛ in.) height, 1965
NPG.66.19

Poet, critic, magazine editor, and novelist Lincoln Kirstein above all played a central role in shaping America's classical ballet tradition. Obsessed with dance from an early age, Kirstein brought choreographer George Balanchine of Russia's Diaghilev Ballet to the United States in the early 1930s, and together they founded the School of American Ballet. Their collaboration continued, and in 1948 they established the New York City Ballet, with Kirstein serving as general director until 1989. He also founded the Dance Archives of the Museum of Modern Art, which became the basis of the Dance Collection of the New York Public Library. The portraitist, Jamie Wyeth, was only nineteen when this painting was completed. AEH

Lincoln Kirstein (1907–1996)

————

Jamie Wyeth (born 1946)
Oil on canvas, 99.1 × 77.8 cm (39 × 30⅝ in.), 1965
Bequest of Lincoln Kirstein
NPG.96.97

Charles Dillon "Casey" Stengel built his reputation as one of baseball's greatest managers by guiding the New York Yankees to ten American League pennants and seven World Series championships in just twelve seasons (1949–60). But it was during his stint as the charismatic shepherd of the fledgling New York Mets (1962–65) that Stengel earned a place in the hearts of baseball lovers everywhere. Unable to budge his hapless team from the National League's cellar, Stengel nonetheless helped the Mets amass legions of loyal fans, thanks to his memorable quips, his tireless zest for the game, and his confident prediction that "the Mets are gonna be amazing." AMS

Casey Stengel (1890–1975)

———

Rhoda Sherbell (born 1933)
Polychromed bronze, 111.8 cm (44 in.) height, with base
1981 cast after 1965 original
NPG.81.67

Beatlemania! It began in the United States when the chords of the band's electrified recordings began blaring from radios across the country. The musicians, four shaggy-haired lads from Liverpool, England, were soon to follow, eager to wow American youth with their guitars and drums. Their single "I Want to Hold Your Hand" was already a number-one hit when the Beatles first stepped onto the tarmac in New York City in February 1964, amid a crescendo of screams from thousands of welcoming fans. The band debuted live on the popular *Ed Sullivan Show* on February 9 and reappeared on the show a week later, in Miami. Meanwhile, they played concerts in Washington, D.C., and at Carnegie Hall in New York. Their stupendous first American tour was merely a prelude to the band's future success.

On September 22, 1967, the Beatles appeared on the cover of *Time* magazine in these mixed-media sculptures by British satirist Gerald Scarfe. His creative interpretations were as original as the Beatles' new album, *Sgt. Pepper's Lonely Hearts Club Band*. This, their eighth album, was a collection of musically complex songs and ballads that radically expanded the genre of pop music. JGB

George Harrison (1943–2001)
Ringo Starr (born 1940)
Paul McCartney (born 1942)
John Lennon (1940–1980)

———————

Gerald Scarfe (born 1936)
Papier-mâché, cloth, wood, metal, and plastic, 121.9 × 55.9 × 45.7 cm
(48 × 22 × 18 in.) grouping, 1967
Time cover, September 22, 1967
Gift of *Time* magazine
NPG.78.TC850

Jimi Hendrix

Jimi Hendrix transformed the creative possibilities of the electric guitar during a short-lived yet influential music career. His use of sound distortion and ear-splitting amplification—together with outrageous showmanship—set him apart from most guitarists of the 1960s. Having taught himself to play by listening to the records of blues guitarists he admired, he formed his first band, the Jimi Hendrix Experience, in London in 1966. Returning to the United States a year later, he became an overnight sensation with his debut album, *Are You Experienced*. On stage, Hendrix displayed extraordinary energy and a frank sexuality that both attracted and unsettled audiences. Yet it was his unconventional rendition of "The Star-Spangled Banner" at the close of the now-legendary Woodstock Festival in 1969 for which he is best remembered today. Hendrix died of a drug overdose a year later, at age twenty-seven. FHG

Jimi Hendrix (1942–1970)

———

Linda McCartney (1942–1998)
Platinum print, 51.3 × 35.3 cm (20³⁄₁₆ × 13⅞ in.), 1967 (printed 1995)
Gift of the photographer, Linda McCartney
NPG.96.26

One of America's most beloved comedians, Bob Hope enjoyed a performing career that lasted more than eight decades. Born in England and raised in Cleveland, Ohio, Hope joined the vaudeville circuit as a teen. By the mid-1930s he was a fixture on radio and a star of such Broadway shows as Cole Porter's *Red, Hot and Blue!* He moved to Hollywood and by 1940 began filming *The Road to Singapore*—the first of the hugely popular series of "*Road*" movies—partnered with golf buddy Bing Crosby. Hope's commitment to entertaining U.S. troops with the USO was legendary, beginning during World War II and ending with the Gulf War. He received five special Academy Awards and, in 1985, a Kennedy Center Honors award. AEH

Bob Hope (1903–2003)

———

Marisol (born 1930)
Polychromed wood, 47 cm (18½ in.) height, 1967
Time cover, December 22, 1967
Gift of *Time* magazine
NPG.78.TC452

Based on a publicity still from Marilyn Monroe's 1953 film *Niagara*, Andy Warhol's portrait of the film star conveys both her glamour and fragility. A gifted performer, Monroe became an iconic sex symbol, entertaining troops in Korea and electrifying movie audiences. Despite her success, she maintained an air of vulnerability. Warhol capitalized on these contradictions, first portraying Monroe after her 1962 death from a drug overdose. Using silkscreens, he created multiple renditions of the actress. By emphasizing the images' off-register printing, Warhol created a powerful metaphor for the dissolution of Monroe's career and the blinding impact of her overexposure. In this screenprint, part of a series of ten, Monroe's sensual features dissolve into a nearly impenetrable mask as Warhol's non-naturalistic colors and their improper alignment produce a jarring effect at once familiar and alienating. ACG

Marilyn Monroe (1926–1962)

———

Andy Warhol (1928–1987)
Screenprint, 91.5 × 91.5 cm (36 × 36 in.), 1967
Gift of Daniel Solomon
NPG.97.51

Richard Nixon owed his election as Dwight Eisenhower's vice president to his early reputation as an anti-Communist. By the time he became president in 1968, however, his thinking had shifted. Under his leadership the confrontational strategies that had long dominated American response to Communism gave way to a historic détente, marked by U.S. recognition of Communist China and better relations with the Soviet Union.

These achievements, however, were eventually overshadowed by disclosure of the Watergate scandals—a web of illegal activity involving scores of Nixon's advisers. Although never implicated in the original crimes, Nixon did become party to attempts to cover them up. Following irrefutable disclosure of that fact, he became the only president ever to resign from office.

Norman Rockwell admitted that he had intentionally flattered Nixon in this portrait. Nixon's appearance was troublesomely elusive, Rockwell noted, and if he was going to err in his portrayal, he wanted it to be in a direction that would please the subject. FSV

Richard M. Nixon (1913–1994)

————

Norman Rockwell (1894–1978)
Oil on canvas, 52.4 × 72.4 cm (20⅝ × 28½ in.), 1968
Donated to the people of the United States of America
by the Richard Nixon Foundation
NPG.72.2

A transformative force in the American labor movement, Cesar Chavez dedicated his life to the struggle to secure fair wages and decent working conditions for the nation's agricultural workers. Chavez had toiled as a migrant in his youth and was well acquainted with the hardships endured by seasonal laborers—many of them Mexican or Mexican American—who followed the harvest on farms throughout California and the Southwest. In 1962, he partnered with activist Dolores Huerta to co-found the forerunner of the United Farm Workers of America (UFW)—the first successful farm workers' union in the nation. In 1965 Chavez initiated a massive boycott of California grapes in a campaign that continued for five years and ended in victory when grape growers agreed to accept unionized field workers. Chavez wears a button displaying the Aztec eagle, the symbol of the UFW. AMS

Cesar Chavez (1927–1993)

————

Manuel Acosta (1921–1989)
Oil on canvas, 61 × 50.8 cm (24 × 20 in.), 1969
Time cover, July 4, 1969
Gift of *Time* magazine
NPG.78.TC298

Concert dancer and choreographer José Limón came to the United States from Mexico in 1915 and began his long career on Broadway in 1928, notably as a leading dancer in the Doris Humphrey–Charles Weidman Company. Like Humphrey and Martha Graham (see p. 156), Limón advocated developing an indigenous American dance, a vision he later pursued with his own company, which he formed in 1946. His first major work, *The Moor's Pavane*, based on Shakespeare's *Othello*, was hailed by critics and won the 1950 *Dance Magazine* Award for achievement in choreography. His later works experimented with abstract themes and sound.

Limón posed for this portrait a few years before his death. The artist, Philip Grausman, evinced a "jeweler's concern for elegant finish," in much of his work and his likeness of the dancer was no exception. AEH

José Limón (1908–1972)

———

Philip Grausman (born 1935)
Bronze, 50.2 cm (19¾ in.) height, 1969
Gift of an anonymous donor
NPG.75.31

The only recipient of two unshared Nobel Prizes—for chemistry and peace—Linus Pauling both advanced science and addressed its social implications. In the 1930s and 1940s, Pauling applied quantum mechanics to chemistry, inspiring new discoveries about molecular structures and leading to his 1954 Nobel Prize. Pauling's resistance to atomic weapons fueled his publication of *No More War!* in 1958 and earned him a second Nobel in 1962. A year later the Nuclear Test-Ban Treaty was implemented.

Alice Neel's informal portrait depicts the scientist outside of the laboratory to indicate the breadth of his commitments. Pauling later explained, "I could have accomplished a lot more science from 1945 to 1965. I decided…I ought to get scientists working for world peace….Scientists have an obligation to help fellow citizens make the right decisions." ACG

Linus Pauling (1901–1994)

———

Alice Neel (1900–1984)
Oil on canvas, 126.4 × 90.2 cm (49¾ × 35½ in.), 1969
NPG.85.73

One of the archetypal heroic figures of twentieth-century film, John Wayne conveyed a decisive, solitary, reverent screen persona that reflected traditional American values. Wayne's collaboration with director John Ford led to such classics as *Stagecoach* (1939), *She Wore a Yellow Ribbon* (1949), and *The Quiet Man* (1952). During World War II, Wayne starred in several morale-boosting movies, including *Flying Tigers* (1942) and *Back to Bataan* (1945). He finally won an Oscar for his portrayal of Rooster Cogburn in *True Grit* (1969). About his long-lived popularity he said, "I play John Wayne in every part regardless of the character, and I've been doing okay, haven't I?" AEH

John Wayne (1907–1979)

———

Harry Jackson (1924–2011)
Polychromed bronze, 73 cm (28¾ in.) height, 1969
Time cover, August 8, 1969
Gift of *Time* magazine
NPG.89.TC17

In 1930 the Gershwin brothers' musical *Girl Crazy* opened on Broadway, and toward the end of the first act, an unknown singer named Ethel Merman mesmerized the audience with her rendition of "I Got Rhythm," in the course of which she held a high C for sixteen bars. As Merman later put it, by the time the applause died, "a star had been born. Me." Over the next five decades, her booming voice and brassy style were the main attraction of some of the most successful Broadway musicals ever, including *Anything Goes, Gypsy*, and *Annie Get Your Gun*—whose score included her trademark song, "There's No Business Like Show Business." Of her singing technique, Merman once said, "I just stand up and holler and hope that my voice holds out."

This image shows Merman dressed for the title role in *Annie Get Your Gun*. AEH

Ethel Merman (1909–1984)

———

Rosemarie Sloat (born 1925)
Oil and acrylic on canvas, 227.3 × 126.4 cm (89½ × 49¾ in.), 1971
Gift of Ethel Merman
NPG.71.50

Writer and political activist Gloria Steinem emerged as a powerful voice for women's rights at a time when many Americans viewed feminism solely as a "white middle-class movement." In provocative articles such as "After Black Power, Women's Liberation" (1969), Steinem argued that inclusiveness across racial and economic boundaries was fundamental to the campaign for gender equality. To underscore the point that all women, regardless of race or class, had a stake in this struggle, Steinem joined forces with leading childcare advocate Dorothy Pitman Hughes. In 1970 they embarked on a series of high-profile national speaking tours to galvanize grassroots support for women's issues. In this formal studio portrait published in *Esquire* magazine in October 1971, Steinem and Hughes signal their solidarity with the raised-fist salute first popularized by members of the Black Power movement. AMS

Gloria Steinem (born 1934)
Dorothy Pitman Hughes (born 1938)

———

Dan Wynn (1919–1995)
Gelatin silver print, 35.4 × 35.5 cm (13¹⁵/₁₆ × 14 in.), 1971
NPG.2005.121

Alex Katz's stylistic hallmarks—the influence of billboard advertising and the cropping of subjects to dramatic effect in particular—could not have been better suited for his portrait of the larger-than-life personality of Bella Abzug. A lawyer and congresswoman, Abzug wore big hats and spoke loudly for the causes she believed in, which encompassed everything from feminism to civil rights. Asked to portray a politician of his liking, Katz picked Abzug as his first choice, and he made this portrait after observing the activist at her office. In a career that spanned more than forty years, Abzug fearlessly threw herself into many of the country's most difficult issues, from Vietnam and McCarthyism to equal rights for gays and lesbians. With its flat planes of color and the banner-like lettering of Abzug's first name, Katz's image captures the political nature of Abzug's persona. AN

Bella Abzug (1920–1988)

————

Alex Katz (born 1927)
Color lithograph, 84.6 × 59.4 cm (33⁵/₁₆ × 23⅜ in.), 1972
NPG.2012.69

Pictured at the Salk Institute for Biological Studies, which he opened in 1963, Jonas Salk built his career on developing vaccines for influenza and polio. In the early 1940s, Salk along with Thomas Francis Jr. revolutionized immunology with their killed-virus vaccine for influenza, which produced the protective antibodies without exposing recipients to the live virus of the disease itself. In 1947 Salk turned to producing a vaccine for polio, a viral infection capable of crippling or killing, especially young children. With the support from what is now the March of Dimes, Salk initiated experiments with killed-virus vaccines, reporting successful results in 1953. By 1955 the efficacy of the vaccine was clear, and it radically diminished the impact of polio in less than a decade. Unwilling to claim a patent, Salk asked rhetorically, "Could you patent the sun?" ACG

Jonas Salk (1914–1995)

———

Arnold Newman (1918–2006)
Gelatin silver print, 23.1 × 34.6 cm (9⅛ × 13⅝ in.), 1975
Gift of Arnold Newman
NPG.91.89.78

Dubbed the "Golden Arm," Johnny Unitas is widely acknowledged to be one of the greatest quarterbacks in professional football history. Unitas led the Baltimore Colts, where he played for seventeen of his eighteen years in the National Football League, to three championships, winning three trophies for Most Valuable Player and invitations to ten Pro Bowl games along the way.

This life portrait of Unitas by Merv Corning—one of the more than three hundred portraits of NFL players that the self-taught artist made beginning in 1967—shows Unitas as many on the field saw him: a leader known for his steely determination and keen strategizing. Commissioned by David Boss, the NFL's pioneering creative director for a quarter of a century, it also reveals the rising significance of image making, marketing, and branding in professional sports. **AN**

Johnny Unitas (1933–2002)

———————

Merv Corning (1926–2006)
Watercolor on paper, 45 × 30 cm (17¹¹⁄₁₆ × 11¹³⁄₁₆ in.), 1975
Partial gift of Carol J. Boss in memory of David A. Boss
NPG.2014.5a

Elvis Presley grew up in the musical melting pot of Memphis, where his emerging talent was heavily influenced by local strains of pop, country, rhythm and blues, and gospel. As a young truck driver in 1953, he paid four dollars to record a song for his mother's birthday. Sun Records—then the label of such other young talents as Johnny Cash and Jerry Lee Lewis—soon signed him, and his first record, "That's All Right, Mama," was an instant hit. By 1956, thanks in part to a series of sensational television appearances, he was crowned the "king of rock and roll," with a string of recordings that included "Heartbreak Hotel," "Don't Be Cruel," and "Hound Dog." Since his death, Presley has emerged as an iconic entertainment figure, and his Graceland mansion has become one of the nation's most-visited popular culture shrines. AEH

Elvis Presley (1935–1977)

———

Ralph W. Cowan (born 1931)
Oil on canvas, 111.8 cm (44 in.) diameter, 1976–88
Gift of R. W. Cowan
NPG.90.114

On being awarded the Nobel Prize for Literature in 1993, Toni Morrison was honored as an author who "in novels characterized by visionary force and poetic import, gives life to an essential aspect of American reality." Drawing upon both her own life and historical accounts, Morrison has crafted stories and essays that speak broadly about such issues as marginality, exclusion, and belonging. A graduate of Howard University, she taught English before becoming an editor at Random House in 1965. There, Morrison helped to develop the careers of several African American authors while simultaneously beginning to publish her own writings.

Helen Marcus created this portrait to help publicize *Song of Solomon*, which was named as a Book-of-the-Month selection, the first such distinction by an African American author since Richard Wright's *Native Son* in 1940. Morrison retired in 2006 after seventeen years on the faculty of Princeton University. FHG

Toni Morrison (born 1931)

———

Helen Marcus (birthdate unknown)
Gelatin silver print, 29.8 × 19.7 cm (11¾ × 7¾ in.), 1978
Gift of Helen Marcus
NPG.2005.107

As a twentieth-century portrait painter, Raphael Soyer continued to work in a realistic vein even as abstraction came to rule the art world. He was noted for his empathetic and sympathetic likenesses, especially of family and friends, such as the poet Allen Ginsberg. Soyer and Ginsberg were part of the post–World War II cultural scene in New York City, and they became friends after meeting in 1965. Ginsberg by then was famous as the author of "Howl"—the quintessential statement of postwar rebellion—and many subsequent works. Soyer signals Ginsberg's poetic career by painting him holding a list that includes "Howl" and "Kaddish." But Soyer really painted this dual portrait to commemorate the poet's long relationship with Peter Orlovsky, with whom he lived and worked for nearly forty years. DCW

Allen Ginsberg (1926–1997)
Peter Orlovsky (1933–2010)

———

Raphael Soyer (1899–1987)
Oil on canvas, 101.6 × 101.6 cm (40 × 40 in.), 1980
Gift of Mary Soyer
NPG.2009.114

In making a portrait, one critic observed, Alice Neel "hurls shafts that hit the mark but do not sting," pinpointing the penetrating yet benevolent quality in the figure studies for which she is best known. Neel adhered to portraiture in the midst of the abstract expressionist movement and was consequently ignored by the art world until shortly before two retrospective exhibitions held during the early 1970s. "Life begins at seventy!" she said of her career's newfound transformation.

In 1975, she began this shocking, endearing, and utterly unconventional self-portrait, which was not completed until 1980. As Neel noted, "The reason my cheeks got so pink was that it was so hard for me to paint that I almost killed myself painting it." A striking challenge to the centuries-old convention of idealized femininity, Neel's only painted self-portrait is wonderfully suggestive of her bohemian, bawdy character. **BBF**

Alice Neel (1900–1984)

———

Self-portrait
Oil on canvas, 135.3 × 101 cm (53¼ × 39¾ in.), 1975–80
NPG.85.19

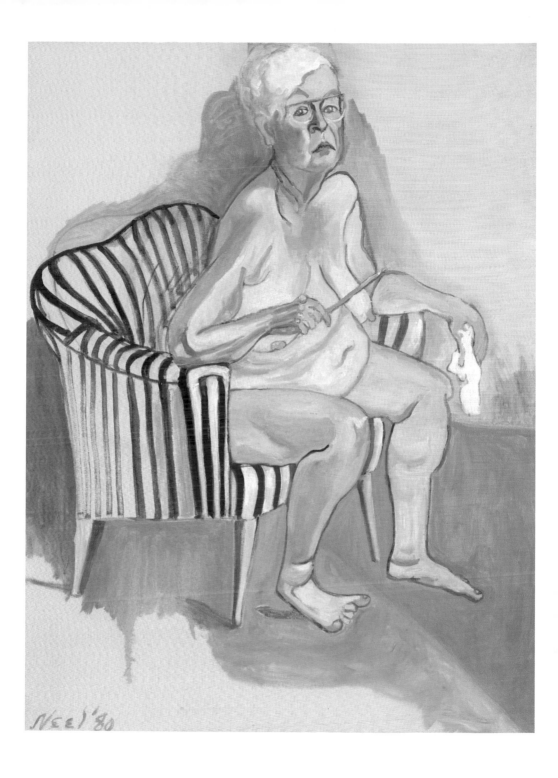

Time magazine placed this portrait of Ronald Reagan on the cover of its 1980 "Man of the Year" issue largely because Reagan had just claimed the White House in the recent November elections. More important, however, the triumph of Reagan's strong conservatism at the polls seemed to signal a marked change in America's political climate, and in his calls for reduced dependence on government, he promised something quite different from recent administrations, Republican and Democratic alike. As *Time* put it, Reagan was not only Man of the Year; he was also "the idea of the year."

For this likeness, *Time* enlisted the services of Aaron Shikler, who has long been considered one of the country's leading traditional portraitists. Among the traits characterizing Shikler's work is a sense of intimacy, which he achieves largely through sensitive lighting. FSV

Ronald Reagan (1911–2004)

———

Aaron Shikler (born 1922)
Oil on paper, approx. 63.5 × 41.3 cm (25 × 16¼ in.), 1980
Time cover, January 5, 1981
Gift of *Time* magazine
NPG.84.TC140

The novel historically has its roots in the city. But the astonishingly prolific John Updike showed how it could also examine the morals and manners of suburban America. In his five-part series whose central character is "Rabbit" Angstrom, Updike chronicled middle-class America's postwar history in comic and heart-breaking fashion. Updike also wrote three novels about a moderately successful Jewish novelist called Henry Bech, who implausibly wins the Nobel Prize; curiously, the Nobel is one prize that Updike did not win.

Updike once said his goal was to publish a book a year, and he came close with his novels and many collections of short stories, poetry, and nonfiction. That ubiquity landed him on the cover of *Time* magazine in 1982. The cover artist was Alex Katz, whose oversize flattened forms, detached expressions, and emphatic patterning had been reinvigorating portrait traditions since the 1960s. WWR/DCW

John Updike (1932–2009)

———

Alex Katz (born 1927)
Oil on canvas, 120.7 × 85.7 cm (47½ × 33¾ in.), 1982
Time cover, October 18, 1982
Gift of *Time* magazine
NPG.84.TC156

For more than a quarter century, Madonna (born Madonna Louise Ciccone) has maintained her standing as a pop music megastar, thanks in large measure to her remarkable talent for reinvention. After a brief career as a professional dancer, she turned to singing and scored a modest hit with her debut album, *Madonna* (1983). But it was her second album, *Like a Virgin* (1984), and her dynamic music videos—viewed by millions on MTV—that transformed the "Material Girl" into an international phenomenon. Madonna courted controversy, sporting underwear as outerwear, accessorizing her look with crucifixes, and delivering over-the-top performances during her sold-out tours. She also earned praise for her film roles in *Desperately Seeking Susan* (1985) and *Evita* (1996). Madonna's extraordinary success paved the way for the next generation of performers, including Lady Gaga and Katy Perry.

Photographing Madonna for the London-based magazine *The Face* in 1983, Kate Simon was struck by the singer's "penetrating gaze and balletic posture" as she posed on a Manhattan rooftop. AMS

Madonna (born 1958)

———

Kate Simon (born 1953)
Gelatin silver print, 23.5 × 15.9 cm (9¼ × 6¼ in.), 1983
NPG.2013.79

With a courageous act of civil disobedience, Rosa Parks sparked a challenge to segregation that culminated in one of the seminal victories of the modern civil rights movement. On December 1, 1955, while traveling on a public bus in Montgomery, Alabama, the seamstress was arrested for refusing the driver's demand that she surrender her seat to a white male passenger. When Parks was convicted of violating local segregation laws, Montgomery's African American community launched a massive one-day boycott of the city's bus system. The boycott expanded with the help of Martin Luther King Jr. (see p. 206) to last 382 days, ending only after the U.S. Supreme Court ruled bus segregation unconstitutional. AMS

Rosa Parks (1913–2005)

———

Marshall D. Rumbaugh (born 1948)
Painted limewood, 99.1 cm (39 in.) height, with base, 1983
NPG.83.163

New Orleans native Antoine "Fats" Domino was already a popular figure in the world of rhythm and blues when his songs such as "Ain't That a Shame" and "Blueberry Hill" (depicted here on the piano) exploded onto the rock-and-roll scene in the 1950s, attracting an enormous popular following.

Artist Red Grooms, who listened to rock and roll in his studio, considers this piece a tribute to Domino. Grooms's interest in three-dimensionality eventually led not only to his construction of huge sculptural pictoramas but also smaller-scale paper sculpture, including innovative printed-and-glued constructions like this exuberant and witty portrait. WWR

Fats Domino (born 1928)

————

Red Grooms (born 1937)
Color lithographic sculpture, approx. 35.6 cm (14 in.), 1984
NPG.2003.78

In the early 1970s, Bruce Springsteen honed his musical chops in North Jersey bars and roadhouses, writing songs and creating a sound that became the anthem for disaffected suburban and working-class Americans. Springsteen's songs like "Born to Run" and "10th Avenue Freezeout," caught the romanticism of rock and roll but also a deep vein of populism in the dignity and respect his music paid to the lives and aspirations of ordinary Americans. Initially dismissed as derivative of Bob Dylan or Van Morrison, Springsteen created music that merged lyrical introspection with a powerhouse sound that made his concerts an ecstatic experience. Simultaneously, *Time* and *Newsweek* covers in 1975 vaulted "The Boss" and his E Street Band to national attention. Springsteen continues to be a powerful presence both in the American songbook and as a performer.

This Annie Leibovitz photograph was reproduced on a poster for Springsteen's "Born in the U.S.A." concert tour in 1984. DCW

Bruce Springsteen (born 1949)

————

Annie Leibovitz (born 1949)
Archival pigment print, 56.1 × 45.6 cm (22 1/16 × 17 15/16 in.), 1984 (printed 2012)
Acquired through the generosity of Hale, Bob, Will, and Meg Krasne
NPG.2013.28

In a prolific yet short-lived career, Jean-Michel Basquiat became a leading figure in the 1980s art world. Having run away from home as a teenager, he supported himself initially by selling homemade postcards and sweatshirts on the street. He emerged as an underground celebrity in 1978, when he and a friend began spray-painting cryptic social messages and the tag SAMO (short for "Same Old Shit") all over Lower Manhattan. Working in a graffiti style, he moved into producing artworks that combined expressively drawn elements like figures and skulls with incisive words and phrases. Soon he was exhibiting at major galleries and museums and collaborating with Andy Warhol. As a black man in a predominantly white art scene, he found himself increasingly caught between a desire for fame and a fear of being exploited by that world. Like his heroes Charlie Parker and Jimi Hendrix (see p. 220), Basquiat burned bright but died young, of a drug overdose. FHG

Jean-Michel Basquiat (1960–1988)

———————

Dmitri Kasterine (born 1932)
Gelatin silver print, 38.3 × 37.7cm (15⅟₁₆ × 14¹³⁄₁₆ in.), 1986
Acquired through the generosity of Norman and Beverly Cox
in honor of their daughter Cara
NPG.2011.24

Supremely talented as a college player at the University of North Carolina at Chapel Hill, which he led to a National Championship in 1982, Michael Jordan inspired the joke: "Who is the only man to hold Michael Jordan to under 20 points a game?" Answer: his coach, the legendary Dean Smith, who favored system over individuals.

Drafted by the Chicago Bulls in 1984, Jordan had the freedom to blossom as a pro, becoming an electrifying scorer with tremendous leaping ability. Despite his individual feats, not until the arrival of another coach with a system, Phil Jackson, did Jordan begin to win championships with the Bulls. Starting in 1991 the Bulls won six NBA titles, and Jordan was chosen as the NBA's Most Valuable Player five times. He was also a fourteen-time All-Star and two-time Olympic gold medalist. Arguably the greatest player of all time, he was inducted into the Basketball Hall of Fame in 2009. Jordan was also in large measure responsible for Nike's breakout from a specialty running shoe manufacturer to a global colossus of sports equipment. He now runs the Charlotte Hornets franchise of the NBA, where he has yet to experience the success he had as a player. DCW

Michael Jordan (born 1963)

———

Annie Leibovitz (born 1949)
Cibachrome print, 36.5 × 27.5 cm (14⅜ × 10¹³⁄₁₆ in.), 1991
NPG.2009.95

Few figures in twentieth-century popular music have exerted more influence than Ray Charles. By developing a style that blended the rhythm and blues tradition with gospel and rock and roll, Charles helped shape the music and style of other performers while creating such timeless hits as "Georgia on My Mind" and "Hit the Road, Jack."

Morgan Monceaux, an amateur musician with no formal training in art, used an innovative mixture of collage technique and found materials to produce a series of portraits of jazz greats. Here, discarded plastic sunglasses signify Charles's blindness, while strips of wood represent piano keys and a microphone stand. Handwritten words surround the figure like an aura, providing biographical details. Monceaux's portraits mirror the improvisational vitality of jazz and honor those musicians like Charles, whom the artist considers "the great rule-breakers of our time." WWR

Ray Charles (1930–2004)

———

Morgan Monceaux (born 1947)
Graphite, pastel, felt-tipped marker, wood, fabric, plastic, and
adhesive on paper, approx. 102.6 × 76.5 cm (40⅜ × 30⅛ in.), 1992–94
Gift of Morgan Monceaux
NPG.2003.81

Armed with superb natural talent, a keen competitive spirit, and poise that set him apart from his rivals, Arthur Ashe made his way from the segregated playground courts of his youth to the pinnacle of the tennis world. Rated among the world's top ten players while still in college, Ashe reached the number-one ranking in spectacular fashion in 1968. After capturing the U.S. amateur title, he served an astonishing twenty-six aces in the final to become the first African American man to claim the U.S. Open championship. Ashe went on to record multiple tournament victories, including his memorable triumph over Jimmy Connors at Wimbledon in 1975. Following a heart attack that forced his retirement in 1980, Ashe dedicated his energies to humanitarian causes. He became a leader in the fight against AIDS in 1992, after revealing that he had contracted the virus through a transfusion. AMS

Arthur Ashe (1943–1993)

———

Louis Briel (born 1945)
Acrylic on canvas, 122 × 81.2 cm (48⅛ × 31¹⁵⁄₁₆ in.), 1993
Gift of the Commonwealth of Virginia and Virginia Heroes, Inc.
NPG.93.101

George H. W. Bush

In the early 1960s, George H. W. Bush presided over a thriving oil business in Houston, Texas, but then he turned to politics. By 1980, when he was elected Ronald Reagan's vice president, he had served as ambassador to the United Nations, envoy to China, and director of the Central Intelligence Agency. In 1988, he won the presidency.

Bush proved sure-footed in foreign policy, where, according to one observer, he was a master of both "timing and substance." More widely traveled than any other president, he managed the policy transitions prompted by the collapse of the Soviet Union and the end of the Cold War. Perhaps his greatest success was the alliance he crafted to thwart Iraq's takeover of Kuwait in 1990.

Bush sat for this portrait at his home in Kennebunkport, Maine. The picture's backdrop, however, is the East Room of the White House. Among artist Ronald Sherr's aims was to balance the formality of the composition with a warmth capable of drawing the viewer into the picture. FSV

George H. W. Bush (born 1924)

———

Ronald Sherr (born 1952)
Oil on canvas, 125.1 × 86.7 cm (49¼ × 34⅛ in.), 1994–95
Gift of Mr. and Mrs. Robert E. Krueger
NPG.95.120

Lionel Hampton began his musical career as a drummer until Louis Armstrong encouraged him to take up the vibraphone in the early 1930s. Hampton introduced that instrument to the jazz idiom and came to the attention of Benny Goodman in 1936. When Goodman formed the Benny Goodman Quartet, Hampton played "vibes" and went on to direct the group's recordings of such favorites as "Dinah" and "Exactly Like You." In 1940 Goodman disbanded the quartet, and Hampton struck out on his own, incorporating such musicians as Charles Mingus, Quincy Jones, and Charlie Parker into the Lionel Hampton Orchestra. Among the top bands in the country, the orchestra played all the popular clubs, as well as Carnegie Hall and Harlem's Apollo Theater. Hampton's high-energy spontaneity was legendary: "We got no routine," he once said. "We just act the way the spirit moves us." AEH

Lionel Hampton (1908–2002)

———

Frederick J. Brown (1945–2012)
Oil on canvas, 244.2 × 182.9 cm (96⅛ × 72 in.), 1997
Gift of Mayor Rudolph Giuliani on behalf of the people of New York
NPG.97.39

Faith Ringgold based her 1998 artist's book, *Seven Passages to a Flight*, and this accompanying quilt on memories drawn from her own childhood in Harlem. Searching for an expression of the African American female experience, she started working in textiles in the 1970s. Her innovative story quilts drew inspiration from Tibetan *tankas*, African piecework, and black American quilting traditions. Long an activist for racial and gender equality, Ringgold used flight here as a metaphor for overcoming the challenges that she encountered as a black woman. "Anyone can fly," she wrote in her award-winning children's book *Tar Beach* (1991). "All you have to do is have somewhere to go that you can't get to any other way." The imagery of flying, Ringgold has explained, "is about achieving a seemingly impossible goal with no more guarantee of success than an avowed commitment to do it." WWR

Faith Ringgold (born 1930)

———

Self-portrait
Quilt with hand-painted etching and pochoir borders on linen
128.4 × 109.3 cm (50⁹⁄₁₆ × 43¹⁄₁₆ in.), 1998
NPG.2004.25

Seven Passages to a Flight

Spike Lee is an innovative and provocative filmmaker with no qualms about confronting hot-button issues of race and class in his feature films and documentaries. In 1986 he scored an indie hit with his first full-length motion picture, *She's Gotta Have It*. Written, directed, and produced by Lee (who also played one of its characters), the film was shot in under two weeks on a budget of $175,000. It earned more than $7 million at the box office. Lee has since brought varied projects to the screen, including *Do the Right Thing* (1989), *Malcolm X* (1992), and *Bamboozled* (2000). His probing documentaries include *4 Little Girls* (1997), an examination of the 1963 bombing of Birmingham's 16th Street Baptist Church, and *When the Levees Broke: A Requiem in Four Acts* (2006), a study of Hurricane Katrina's devastating impact on New Orleans. Seen here with his camera at the ready, Lee shades his eyes while returning our gaze. AMS

Spike Lee (born 1957)

———

Jesse Frohman (born 1958)
Inkjet print, 80.1 × 78.7 cm (31⁹⁄₁₆ × 31 in.), 1999 (printed 2014)
Gift of Jesse Frohman
NPG.2015.6

Pedro Martinez was told that he was too small to be a major-league power pitcher, yet from his first appearance he consistently overpowered the best hitters in the world. He won three Cy Young Awards in a span of four seasons and retired in 2011 with a record of 219 wins and only 100 losses. In 2000, the very heart of the home-run/steroid era, Martinez had an earned-run average of 1.74—more than three runs a game less than the American League average; he allowed only seventeen home runs in 217 innings pitched. Baseball authority Peter Gammons believes that "Pedro's seven-year period, 1997–2003, was the most dominant stretch of any pitcher in baseball history." Martinez is also widely applauded for his commitment to advancing opportunities for less fortunate children in his native Dominican Republic and in the United States, where he is a naturalized citizen.

Susan Miller-Havens titled this portrait *El Orgullo y Determinación (Pride and Determination)* as a statement of Martinez's accomplishment in overcoming obstacles and becoming one of the most dominant pitchers of baseball's modern era. SH

Pedro Martinez (born 1971)

———

Susan Miller-Havens (born 1944)
Oil and beeswax on birch panel, 144.8 × 53.3 cm (57 × 21 in.), 2000
Gift of Gloria Trowbridge Gammons and Peter Warren Gammons
in honor of Pedro Martinez
NPG.2010.85

A distinguished biochemist, Maxine Singer earned the National Medal of Science in 1992 and led the Carnegie Institution from 1988 to 2002. Her groundbreaking research on DNA has improved our understanding of the development and structure of such genetic diseases as hemophilia. Singer notes that such experimentation, for which she helped devise ethical guidelines, "bring[s] closer the day when the ability to manipulate genetic material can be used for improving the lives of all humans."

Jon Friedman's study for a portrait commissioned by the Carnegie Institution reflects Singer's wide-ranging interests, from DNA to astronomy. Her influential *Genes and Genomes* (1990, with Paul Berg) appears beside a model of the Carnegie's Giant Magellan Telescope. Her family is pictured in the lower left, while Singer encourages two youngsters in the image directly below her book, illustrating her commitment to science education and public service. ACG

Maxine Singer (born 1931)

———

Jon Friedman (born 1947)
Charcoal on paper, 123.9 × 78.1 cm (48 ¾ × 30 ¾ in.), 2001
NPG.2005.54

Forty years ago Diane von Fürstenburg designed the iconic wrap dress that continues to captivate women from Madonna (see p. 262) to Michelle Obama, Beyoncé to Kate Middleton. With its zipperless, buttonless construction, the dress allows its liberated wearer to move comfortably from home to the workplace to the evening and still look powerful, polished, and feminine. Von Fürstenberg said in the *Los Angeles Times*, "It's the dress that… paid all my bills, gave me my fame and allowed me to be free." Born in Belgium to Jewish parents, von Fürstenberg credits her mother, a former prisoner in the Auschwitz concentration camp, for teaching her that "fear is not an option." Von Fürstenberg and artist Anh Duong share a bond as feminists. Duong began the portrait, which is titled *Cosmogony of Desire*, by painting one eye on the canvas and then worked the rest of the body around it. Von Fürstenberg noticed that in that one eye, "she completely and totally captured me." DDM

Cosmogony of Desire
Diane von Fürstenberg (born 1946)

———

Anh Duong (born 1960)
Oil on canvas, 243.8 × 182.9 cm (96 × 72 in.), 2001
Gift of Diane von Fürstenberg
NPG.2015.3

The visionary co-founder of Apple, Steve Jobs was the modern-day version of an earlier era's Thomas Edison: beginning with the MacIntosh computer, his innovations generated a cultural revolution in everyday life. In 1976 he and Steve Wozniak founded Apple and began producing personal computers. After losing a power struggle in 1985, Jobs left Apple and later acquired Pixar Animation Studios, where he produced a string of films such as *Toy Story*. He returned to Apple in 1996 and launched an era of extraordinary inventiveness. With spellbinding showmanship, Jobs set out to "make a dent in the universe" and over the next several years introduced the iPod, the iPhone, and the iPad—products that transformed the consumer electronics industry. His entrepreneurship stressed design, and Apple products are known for their functional elegance. Jobs once said: "Most people make the mistake of thinking design is what it looks like…. Design is how it works." AEH

Steve Jobs (1955–2011)

———

Diana Walker (born 1942)
Digital inkjet print, 24.7 × 36.9 cm (9¾ × 14½ in.), 2004 (printed 2011)
Gift of Diana Walker
NPG.2011.42

Artist Mickalene Thomas created a double portrait of Oprah Winfrey and Condoleeza Rice (not pictured) to emphasize how both African American women overcame obstacles throughout their lives. For Winfrey, Thomas uses her characteristic rhinestones to highlight the multimedia mogul's megawatt smile and verve. Winfrey's confident gaze affirms her bona fide celebrity status. Winfrey catapulted to fame in 1986 with her self-named talk show, a daily telecast that ran for twenty-five years and won multiple awards. Winfrey always connected with her subjects, whether she interviewed famous people or ordinary citizens. Building on the devotion of viewers everywhere, she turned to recommending books, promoting self-help, and creating HARPO studios, a magazine, and a television network. Born impoverished to a single mother from rural Mississippi, she has become an influential media leader and philanthropist. She has also given acclaimed performances in *The Color Purple* (1985) and *The Butler* (2013). Awarded the Presidential Medal of Freedom in 2013, Winfrey recently produced *Selma*, a movie about the 1965 marches from Selma to Montgomery, Alabama, in support of voting rights for African Americans. AN

Oprah Winfrey (born 1954)

———————

Mickalene Thomas (born 1971)
Screenprint with hand-applied rhinestones on four-ply board
71.1 × 81 cm (28 × 31⅞ in.), 2007–8
NPG.2013.13.1

Lincoln Schatz's generative portraits of nineteen leading American innovators, known collectively as *Esquire's Portrait of the Twenty-First Century*, were created in 2008 on commission from the magazine. Each of these sitters—representing leadership in the realms of business, medicine, science, technology, and the arts—sat for his or her portrait for one hour in the artist's ten-by-ten-foot "Cube," during which time they participated in activities of personal interest. The Cube is embedded with twenty-four cameras, each of which recorded the sitter from a different angle. The ever-changing generative portrait that results consists of the footage from each camera played back for different durations and in different sequences, creating a representation that is analogous to a personal encounter with these individuals.

Academy Award–winning actor and director George Clooney is one of the leading screen stars of his generation. He is depicted in his Cube portrait dancing with a series of women, including the artist's mother. ACG

George Clooney (born 1961)

———

Lincoln Schatz (born 1963)
Digital file, 2008
Gift of Lincoln Schatz
NPG.2010.119.17

Bill Gates dropped out of Harvard to write software for the earliest personal computers. His company, Microsoft, developed a computer operating system for wide-scale nontechnical use that spurred on the personal computer revolution begun in the 1980s. Microsoft remains a leader in the industry and made Gates among the world's wealthiest individuals. Melinda French Gates has degrees in computer science, economics, and business, and was employed by Microsoft before marrying Bill Gates in 1994.

The couple created the Bill & Melinda Gates Foundation with the mission of helping all people live healthy, productive lives. Global priorities include improving health and boosting the productivity of small farms in poor countries; national initiatives include implementing partnerships to make sure students graduate from high school ready for college and helping local libraries provide free computer and Internet services.

The painting is set near the Gates family home on Lake Washington, near Seattle. The collaged screen on the left includes maps, charts, and images referencing the foundation's work, with the statement "All Lives Have Equal Value." The background shows the lake with the Olympic Mountains in the distance. SH/BBF

Bill Gates (born 1955)
Melinda French Gates (born 1964)

———

Jon Friedman (born 1947)
Oil and collage on canvas attached to wood panel
127.6 × 117.5 cm (50¼ × 46¼ in.), 2010
Acquired through the Marc Pachter Commissioning Fund
NPG.2010.83

Deborah Kass has been one of the most consistently innovative and productive artists of the post–pop art era. Early in her career, Kass, following Andy Warhol, became interested in appropriation: adapting and altering other works of art to elaborate on—and change—the art historical tradition. In *Red Deb* (shown here), *Yellow Deb*, *Silver Deb*, and *Blue Deb*, she models her self-portrait on Warhol's screenprints of celebrities surrounded by resplendently colored backgrounds. In some respects the self-portraits closely imitate Warhol's 1964 print of Elizabeth Taylor, but Kass's subtle shifts change the meaning to reflect her own themes: her gender, Jewishness, and sexuality. In repurposing Warhol's style, she challenges the male-dominated art world; in choosing Taylor, she plays on the actress's WASP background and conversion to Judaism; and in borrowing the heavy makeup, she implies an ironic, hyper-girlish reference to her lesbianism. WWR

Deborah Kass (born 1952)

———

Self-portrait
Screenprint, 61.5 × 61.5 cm (24³⁄₁₆ × 24³⁄₁₆ in.), 2012
Acquired through the Abraham and Virginia Weiss
Charitable Trust, Amy and Marc Meadows
C/NPG.2013.75.1

The son of Jamaican immigrants, retired four-star general Colin L. Powell decided on a military career while at City College of New York. He served in Vietnam, earning a Purple Heart and Bronze Star. A White House Fellowship brought him to the attention of Caspar Weinberger, who made Powell his aide upon becoming President Ronald Reagan's secretary of defense. While there, Powell helped to coordinate the invasion of Granada and bombing of Libya in 1986. Powell became national security advisor in 1987 and chairman of the Joint Chiefs of Staff in 1991 and helped plan Operation Desert Storm. There, he enunciated what became known as the "Powell doctrine" of using "decisive force" to maximize success and minimize casualties, a reformulation of strategy resulting from the army's unhappiness with the way in which the United States fought the Vietnam War. In 2001 President George W. Bush appointed Powell to be the first African American secretary of state.

After visiting a number of sites relevant to Powell's career, artist Ronald Sherr placed him in front of Theodore Roosevelt Hall at the National War College at Fort McNair in Washington, D.C. SH

Colin Powell (born 1937)

———

Ronald Sherr (born 1952)
Oil on canvas, 235 × 131.4 cm (92½ × 51¾ in.), 2012
Supported by a grant from the Donald W. Reynolds Foundation
and by the Marc Pachter Commissioning Fund
NPG.2012.16

One of America's most important writers and poets, Maya Angelou wrote a series of seven autobiographical novels that are an indelible record of resistance and achievement by African Americans, particularly African American women. Angelou had a difficult and endangered childhood, shuttling back and forth between relatives in the North and South. She suffered from economic hardship and sexual abuse, which she documented in her first book, *I Know Why the Caged Bird Sings* (1969), and in subsequent volumes. Her subject was always her own life, and her autobiographies are not necessarily strictly factual or literally "true," but rather a retelling of emotional truths. A politically engaged writer, Angelou was also a poet; she read her poem "On the Pulse of the Morning" at President Bill Clinton's 1993 inauguration. DCW

Maya Angelou (1928–2014)

———

Ross Rossin (born 1964)
Oil on canvas, 121.9 × 121.9 cm (48 × 48 in.), 2013
Gift of Andrew J. Young Foundation
NPG.2014.2

A familiar face on screen since the late 1980s, Brad Pitt won a Golden Globe Award for his role as a patient in the psychological thriller *Twelve Monkeys* (1995). Nominated for four Academy Awards, he served as a producer on *12 Years a Slave* (2013), which won a Best Picture Oscar.

Colin Davidson's portrait of Irish singer-songwriter Glen Hansard caught Pitt's eye when he saw it reproduced on an album cover. On several occasions, the actor and artist met in London, Surrey, and Buckinghamshire, where they spent time together painting and talking. During these sessions, Davidson began a series of portraits of Pitt, including this one, made just before Pitt cut his hair short for the filming of *Fury* (2014). The glassy, introspective eyes are typical of Davidson's noncommissioned portraits as he seeks "a certain vulnerable quality" and desires to capture his subjects "lost in thought," removed from their celebrity personas as seen through the mass media. DDM

Brad Pitt (born 1963)

———

Colin Davidson (born 1968)
Oil on canvas, 127 × 116.8 cm (50 × 46 in.), 2013
Gift of the Lowry Wallace Collection, Ireland
NPG.2014.101

As an undergraduate student at Yale University, Maya Lin redefined the conventional notion of a heroic war monument with her understated and controversial design for the Vietnam Veterans Memorial, dedicated in 1982. Although still best-known for that memorial, Lin is an internationally recognized artist and architect whose work also includes large-scale, site-specific installations such as *Storm King Wavefield*. A committed environmentalist, Lin explores how we relate and respond to the environment and presents new ways of seeing the world, for example blurring the boundaries between two- and three-dimensional space. Artist Karin Sander's diminutive three-dimensional scanned portrait appropriately depicts Lin at a 1:5 scale, reflecting the architect's sense of herself as a small part of a global environment. Like so many of Lin's own designs, the unconventionality of this portrait invites the viewer to look more closely and see the subject in a new way. EHJ

Maya Lin (born 1959)

———

Karin Sander (born 1957)
3-D bodyscan from life, polychrome 3-D inkjet print, plaster material, pigment ink, black and white, 1:5 scale, 33 cm (13 in.) height, 2014
Acquired through the generosity of Academy of Achievement/ Wayne and Catherine Reynolds
NPG.2015.15

Measurements

Unless otherwise noted, measurements indicate stretcher size for paintings, plate sizes for daguerreotypes and ambrotypes, and sheet sizes for works on paper

Index of Sitters

Index of Artists

This book may be purchased for educational, business, or sales promotional use. For information, please write: Special Markets Department, Smithsonian Books, P. O. Box 37012, MRC 513, Washington, DC 20013

Published by Smithsonian Books in association with the National Portrait Gallery, Smithsonian Institution

Director: Carolyn Gleason
Production Editor: Christina Wiginton
Project Manager: Dru Dowdy, Head of Publications, National Portrait Gallery
Edited by Lise Sajewski
Designed by Studio A

Library of Congress Cataloging-in-Publication Data
National Portrait Gallery (Smithsonian Institution)
Portrait of a nation.—Second edition.
pages cm
Summary: "The National Portrait Gallery, which averages one million visits per year, is dedicated to the exhibition and study of portraits of people who have made significant contributions to American history and culture. It is the only museum of its kind in the United States to reflect the connection between American history, biography, and art"—Provided by publisher.
Includes bibliographical references and index.
ISBN 978-1-58834-407-6 (paperback)
1. Portraits, American—Catalogs. 2. United States—Biography—Portraits—Catalogs. 3. Portraits—Washington (D.C.)—Catalogs. 4. National Portrait Gallery (Smithsonian Institution)—Catalogs. I. Title.
N857.8.A64 2015
757.0972—dc23   2015012959

21 20 19 18 17   6 5 4 3 2

The winner of thirty-nine Grand Slam singles, doubles, and mixed-doubles titles (including twenty Wimbledon crowns), tennis great Billie Jean King has long championed gender equity both on and off the court. King made her Wimbledon debut in 1961, and by 1966 she was tennis's top-ranked American player. In 1968—the first year that Wimbledon opened competition to professionals as well as amateurs—King turned professional and captured the All-England singles and doubles titles. Frustrated that professional tennis staged few women's matches and that the prize money women received was a fraction of that bestowed upon male players, King helped launch the Virginia Slims Circuit for women's tennis in 1970. She became a founding member and first president of the Women's Tennis Association in 1973. That year she struck a blow for women everywhere by trouncing former tennis champion and self-proclaimed male chauvinist Bobby Riggs in the match touted as the "Battle of Sexes." AMS

Billie Jean King (born 1943)

Lynn Gilbert (born 1938)
Gelatin silver print, 24.5 × 16.4 cm (9⅝ × 6⁷⁄₁₆ in.), 1979
NPG.2014.13

In the early stages of the 1976 presidential campaign, the experts hardly gave a second thought to James Earl "Jimmy" Carter's chances of winning the Democratic nomination, much less the White House. But the former Georgia governor's image as a Washington outsider, along with his traditional populism, had great voter appeal, and in the final poll he emerged triumphant. Unfortunately, Carter did not prove as popular in the presidency as he had on the stump, being blamed for problems such as runaway inflation. Nevertheless, his administration had some unalloyed successes, including a landmark peace agreement between Egypt and Israel, which would probably never have been reached without Carter's own dogged determination to make it happen.

Artist Robert Templeton made the first sketches for this portrait at the White House in 1978. In the picture, Carter stands in the Oval Office, which is furnished as it had been during his administration. The donkey statuette on his desk was a gift from the Democratic National Committee. FSV

Jimmy Carter (born 1924)

———

Robert Templeton (1929–1991)
Oil on canvas, 232.4 × 142.2 cm (91½ × 56 in.), 1980
Partial gift of the 1977 Inauguration Committee
NPG.84.154